# HEALING GOUT COOKBOOK

*1200-Days of Easy, Healthy and Delicious Recipes to Manage Gout, Lower Uric Acid Levels, and Reduce Body Inflammation. Includes 30-Day Meal Plan*

**Elliana Hughes**

# Table of Contents

| | | |
|---|---|---|
| INTRODUCTION | | 5 |
| WHAT IS GOUT? | | 5 |
| WHAT CAUSES GOUT? | | 6 |
| GOUT SYMPTOMS | | 6 |
| THE STAGES OF GOUT | | 6 |
|     1.1.1 | *Stage 1: The Hyperuricemia* | 7 |
|     1.1.2 | *Stage 2: Acute Attack Of Gout* | 7 |
|     1.1.3 | *Stage 3: The Inter Critical Phase* | 7 |
|     1.1.4 | *Stage 4: Chronic Gout* | 8 |
| FOODS TO EAT | | 8 |
| FOODS TO EAT IN MODERATION | | 10 |
| FOODS TO AVOID | | 10 |
| PHYSICAL ACTIVITY | | 11 |
| **CHAPTER 1: BREAKFAST** | | **12** |
| 1. | Raspberry Oatmeal Bars | 12 |
| 2. | Pistachio Smoothie | 12 |
| 3. | Broccoli Spinach Frittatas | 12 |
| 4. | Turkey Hash | 13 |
| 5. | Almond Granola | 13 |
| 6. | Apple Cinnamon Oats | 14 |
| 7. | Sweet Potato Orange Smoothie | 14 |
| 8. | Banana Oatmeal | 14 |
| 9. | Orange Oatmeal Muffins | 15 |
| 10. | Coconut Strawberry Porridge | 15 |
| 11. | Banana Coconut Pancakes | 15 |
| 12. | Banana Date Porridge | 16 |
| 13. | Apple-Cinnamon Smoothie | 16 |
| 14. | Fruity Breakfast Bars | 16 |
| 15. | Artichoke Egg Casserole | 17 |
| 16. | Coconut Chocolate Oatmeal | 17 |
| 17. | Poppy Oatmeal Cups | 18 |
| 18. | Pumpkin Porridge | 18 |
| 19. | Blueberry Quinoa Porridge | 18 |
| 20. | Sweet Potato Casserole | 19 |
| 21. | Raspberry Pineapple Smoothie | 19 |
| 22. | Beef Breakfast | 19 |
| 23. | Triple Berry Oats | 20 |
| 24. | Pancake Bites | 20 |
| 25. | Tofu Scramble | 21 |
| 26. | Spicy Quinoa | 21 |
| 27. | Black Bean Breakfast | 22 |
| 28. | Tomatoes Egg Scramble | 22 |
| 29. | Coconut Pancakes | 23 |
| 30. | Overnight Muesli | 23 |
| **CHAPTER 2: VEGETARIAN** | | **23** |
| 31. | Boiled Beans | 23 |
| 32. | Quinoa With Pepperoncini | 24 |
| 33. | Minestrone Soup | 24 |
| 34. | Basic Quinoa | 24 |
| 35. | Baked Spiced Tofu | 25 |
| 36. | Spiced Sweet Potato Soup | 25 |
| 37. | Coconutty Brown Rice | 26 |
| 38. | Thai Vegetable Soup | 26 |
| 39. | Butter Chickpeas | 26 |
| 40. | Wild Rice Mushroom Soup | 27 |
| 41. | Sweet Potato Leek Soup | 27 |
| 42. | Spaghetti Squash | 27 |
| 43. | Baked Navy Beans | 28 |
| 44. | Cauliflower Rice Risotto | 28 |
| 45. | Harvest Rice | 28 |
| 46. | Vegetable Broth | 29 |
| 47. | Grain-Free Salad Bowl | 29 |
| 48. | Stuffed Sweet Potatoes | 30 |
| 49. | Split Pea Carrot Soup | 30 |
| 50. | Spanish Rice | 30 |
| 51. | Fried Quinoa | 31 |
| 52. | Mushroom Risotto | 31 |
| **CHAPTER 3: FISH AND SEAFOODS** | | **31** |
| 53. | Basic Shrimp | 31 |
| 54. | Mediterranean Fish Stew | 32 |
| 55. | Tuna Salad With Brown Rice | 32 |
| 56. | Lemon Dill Salmon | 33 |
| 57. | Power Poke Bowl | 33 |
| 58. | Seared Citrus Scallops With Mint And Basil | 34 |
| 59. | Seared Cod With Mushroom Sauce | 34 |
| 60. | Seafood Stew | 35 |
| 61. | Herbed Salmon Orzo Antipasto | 35 |
| 62. | Rainbow Trout | 36 |
| 63. | Buckwheat Ramen With Cod | 36 |
| 64. | Shrimp Balls Over Garlicky Greens | 37 |
| 65. | Shrimp Paella | 37 |
| 66. | Garlic Shrimp And Broccoli | 38 |
| **CHAPTER 4: CHICKEN AND POULTRY** | | **39** |
| 67. | Chicken Tenders With Mustard Sauce | 39 |
| 68. | Chicken Breasts With Mushrooms | 39 |
| 69. | Rosemary Chicken | 40 |

| 70. | Jerk Chicken | 40 |
|---|---|---|
| 71. | Spiced Chicken Vegetables | 40 |
| 72. | Chicken Adobo | 41 |
| 73. | Chicken Cacciatore | 41 |
| 74. | Turkey Meatloaf | 42 |
| 75. | Avocado Chicken Salad | 42 |
| 76. | Tuscan Chicken | 43 |
| 77. | Turkey With Bell Peppers And Rosemary | 43 |
| 78. | Gingered Turkey Meatballs | 44 |
| 79. | Chicken Stir-Fry | 44 |
| 80. | Turkey Sweet Potato Hash | 44 |
| 81. | Whole Roasted Chicken | 45 |
| 82. | Easy Chicken And Broccoli | 45 |
| 83. | Coconut Lime Chicken With Cauliflower | 45 |
| 84. | Italian Seasoned Turkey Breast | 46 |
| 85. | Chicken Sandwiches With Roasted Red Pepper Aioli 46 | |
| 86. | Turkey Kale Fry | 47 |
| 87. | Ground Turkey And Spinach Stir-Fry | 47 |
| 88. | Chicken And Cauliflower Bake | 47 |
| 89. | Chicken, Mushrooms, And Quinoa | 48 |
| 90. | Garlic Turkey Breast | 48 |
| 91. | Lime Chicken And Rice | 49 |
| 92. | Turkey Burgers | 49 |
| 93. | Chicken Bell Pepper Sauté | 50 |

**CHAPTER 5: MEAT** .................................................. 50

| 94. | Fried Beef And Bell Pepper | 50 |
|---|---|---|
| 95. | Chili-Lime Pork Loin | 50 |
| 96. | Beef Broth | 51 |
| 97. | Ground Beef Chili With Tomatoes | 51 |
| 98. | Pork Ragù | 51 |
| 99. | Beefy Lentil Stew | 52 |
| 100. | Beef And Bell Pepper Fajitas | 52 |
| 101. | Beef Meatloaf | 52 |
| 102. | Fried Beef And Broccoli | 53 |
| 103. | Hamburgers | 53 |
| 104. | Beef Tenderloin | 53 |
| 105. | Herbed Meatballs | 54 |
| 106. | Bolognese Sauce | 54 |
| 107. | Mustard Pork Tenderloin | 55 |
| 108. | Beef Steak Tacos | 55 |

**CHAPTER 6: SNACKS AND SIDES** ................................. 55

| 109. | Pickled Vegetables | 55 |
|---|---|---|
| 110. | Chickpea Smash | 56 |
| 111. | Cauliflower Rice With Beans | 56 |
| 112. | Green Smoothie Bowl | 56 |
| 113. | Cucumber And Bulgur Salad | 57 |
| 114. | Yogurt With Dates | 57 |
| 115. | Zucchini Fritters | 57 |
| 116. | Pickled Shiitake | 58 |
| 117. | Bean Salsa | 58 |
| 118. | Maple Collard Greens | 59 |
| 119. | Toasted Nut Mix | 59 |
| 120. | Flaxseed Power Bites | 59 |
| 121. | Brussels Sprouts With Walnuts | 60 |
| 122. | Sweet Potato Mash | 60 |
| 123. | Cinnamon Applesauce | 61 |
| 124. | Pico De Gallo | 61 |
| 125. | Fennel Cabbage Slaw | 61 |
| 126. | Citrus Spinach | 62 |

**CHAPTER 7: DESSERT** ............................................... 62

| 127. | Peach-Raspberry Crumble | 62 |
|---|---|---|
| 128. | Ginger Jam Dots | 63 |
| 129. | Almond Butter Mini Muffins | 63 |
| 130. | Apple Cinnamon Muesli | 63 |
| 131. | Almond-Orange Torte | 64 |
| 132. | Blueberry Cobbler | 64 |
| 133. | Chai Pudding | 65 |
| 134. | Spice Stuffed Apple Bake | 65 |
| 135. | Banana Cacao Brownies | 65 |
| 136. | Coconut Hot Chocolate | 66 |
| 137. | Quinoa With Raspberries | 66 |
| 138. | Chia Pudding With Cherries | 66 |
| 139. | Brownies With Strawberry Sauce | 67 |
| 140. | Berry Pops | 67 |
| 141. | Banana Pops | 67 |
| 142. | Chocolate Tofu Pudding | 68 |
| 143. | Strawberry Granita | 68 |
| 144. | Chocolate Bark | 69 |
| 145. | Glazed Pears With Hazelnuts | 69 |
| 146. | Mango-Peach Yogurt | 69 |
| 147. | Almond Butter Fudge | 70 |
| 148. | Berry And Chia Yogurt | 70 |
| 149. | Blueberry Coconut Muffins | 71 |
| 150. | Figs Apple Compote | 71 |

**CHAPTER 8: 30-DAY MEAL PLAN** ................................ 72

**CONCLUSION** ........................................................... 74

**INDEX** ..................................................................... 75

# Introduction

Gout is a disease in which the affected person suffers from repeated attacks of inflammatory arthritis, mainly in the joints & lower limbs. Nowadays, gout affects roughly 1 to 2% of the population in the US (particularly males). But unfortunately, that number is steadily increasing. Additional symptoms of gout and severe pain in the affected areas include joint swelling, fatigue, fever & an increased risk of even more unbearable kidney stones.

As with any illness or medical requirement, people with gout should lead a lifestyle that minimizes the amount of pain they experience from the disease. One such lifestyle modification should be a change in diet, as some foods can aggravate gout while others can relieve it.

The most harmful foods for gout are that is a significant amount of purine, like seafood, bread & red meats; because purine is made up of uric acids that, if discharged into the body, will only boost the swelling around the joints & thus cause the pain worse.

On the other hand, antipurine foods allow you to enjoy a delicious meal while avoiding ingredients that can worsen your pain. If you've been suffering from gout for too long and need to find foods you can enjoy while minimizing the pain, you've come to the right place. We will describe and detail hundreds of gout recipes that do just that.

As Gout is a health condition and affects a lot of people, it can affect your quality of life, and it can also cause a person pain.

One of the best ways to avoid gout is to eat healthy food. Though these are both important, there are many other ways you can help prevent or reduce gout from happening.

## What Is Gout?

Gout is a painful form of arthritis that may present as acute or chronic swelling in the hands or feet. It has historically been considered "the disease of kings." Gout was first discovered by the Egyptians in 2640 BC and was thought to be triggered by the excessive consumption of rich foods and alcohol that only the wealthy could afford. The word gout comes from the Latin word gutta ("drop"). It relates to the perpetuating belief in the four "humors," an ancient Greek medical term for the liquids that they believed influenced health: blood, phlegm, yellow bile, and black bile. When in balance, the humors would maintain good health, but under certain conditions, they could move, or "drop," into a joint, creating inflammation and pain. In some eras, gout was seen as desirable by the politically and socially powerful because it implied having money to spend on fine food and wine.

Medical professionals have been treating gout for centuries. While the majority of gout patients are men between the ages of 30 and 50, women are also susceptible to gout, particularly after menopause. The risk for developing gout is based on two main factors: genetic makeup and an excess of uric acid production in the blood from the foods we eat. While we can't alter our genetic makeup, we can manage the types of foods we eat and make conscious decisions that will help prevent flare-ups. Uric acid is produced when the body breaks down purines. When uric acid levels keep on going high, uric acid crystals form, and the excess buildup of crystals causes painful inflammation in the joints.

## What Causes Gout?

The human body produces uric acid when it breaks down chemicals named purines discovered in particular drinks & foods. This standard by-product passes via the kidneys & leaves the body during urination.

Periodically the body constructs extensive uric acid. Or the kidneys are failing. When the body has an elevated amount of uric acid or hyperuricemia, uric acid crystals can accumulate in the joints. Sharp needle crystals cause gout. However, numerous people with higher uric acid levels never develop gout.

## Gout Symptoms

An attack of gout is called a gout attack. It is excruciating and can come on suddenly, often at night. During a gout attack, symptoms in the affected joints may include:
- Redness.
- Stiffness.
- Intense pain.
- Swelling.
- Tenderness, even to light touch, like from a bed sheet.
- Warmth or a sensation like the joint is "on the conflagration.

## The Stages of Gout

Like so many diseases, gout also has stages and certain characteristics can be used to tell which stage the gout is in. Because, to put it plainly and clearly, you can live with gout not just for years, but for decades. But it can progress differently. And it is precisely these differentiations that I would like to present here at this point.

### 1.1.1 Stage 1: The Hyperuricemia

In hyperuricemia, i.e. in the first stage, the level of uric acid is merely increased. When we speak of increased here, then, in numerical terms, it is more than 6.5 milligrams per 100 milliliters in the blood serum. Normal, however, would be a value of 3 to 6 milligrams per 100 milliliters. If this is the case, then by definition we are talking about hyperuricemia. However, this condition is not yet drastically noticeable and can therefore last for years without the person noticing anything. At this stage there is only an excess of acid, but the first crystals can already form here. These then develop into semolina, which in turn can become stones. Here we come to stage 2.

### 1.1.2 Stage 2: Acute Attack Of Gout

In principle, one can say that the higher the uric acid level, the greater the risk of an acute gout attack. This manifests itself in pain in the individual joints. This often begins in the so-called base joints of the extremities, e.g. B. the toes. Here mainly the big toe. After that, the other joints, ascending the ankle and knees, are usually affected. This occurs less often in the hands and arms. If such an attack of gout is not treated, it usually lasts from a few hours to a few days.

Most patients can be treated quickly, however, as this pain can be very uncomfortable. After that, however, the symptoms subside. Therefore also declared as a seizure. Sometimes this pain is accompanied by reddening and/or swelling of the joint, possibly also an unusual warming. In some cases there is also a sensitivity to touch. Sometimes palpitations, nausea with and without vomiting, headache and fever were also observed.

Often there was also a subjectively reduced performance and this attack usually occurs at night, at least in the initial phase. These are all side effects of the stage two seizure. Treated with medication, the duration of the attack can be shortened. If the gout is not treated, the mobility of the affected joints decreases. This results in poor walking and grasping. These are becoming increasingly difficult. When this point is reached, we come to the next phase.

### 1.1.3 Stage 3: The Inter Critical Phase

What does inter critical phase mean? What is meant here is the time between two attacks. Initially, these seizures occur at irregular intervals. At this stage of the inter critical phase, those affected are symptom-free, but this does not mean that the uric acid level is falling. It is still high, only the inflammatory, painful processes do not occur. In this phase, these only come in spurts. He will bear this in the next phase.

### 1.1.4 *Stage 4: Chronic Gout*

In the chronic gout stage, there are also symptoms between attacks. In this case, complaints include pain as well as restrictions in freedom of movement. Here one speaks of chronic gout.

## Foods To Eat

**Dairy**

- Egg substitutes
- Low-fat cottage cheese
- Skim or 1% milk
- Coffee
- Seltzer

**Fats**

- Corn oil
- Olive oil
- Sesame oil

**Fish/Seafood**

- Flounder
- Salmon
- Sole
- Tilapia

**Fruits**

- Apricots
- Bananas
- Cherries
- Grapes
- Melon (cantaloupe, honeydew, watermelon)
- Peaches
- Raisins

**Grains**

- Eggs
- Low-fat cheese
- Low-fat yogurt

**Drinks**

- Tea
- Water
- Canola oil
- Grapeseed oil
- Peanut oil
- Walnut oil
- Catfish
- Red snapper
- Sea bass
- Swai (aka basa)
- Whitefish
- Apples
- Avocados
- Berries (blackberries, blueberries, raspberries, strawberries)
- Citrus fruits (grapefruit, oranges, mandarins)
- Kiwi
- Nectarines
- Pears
- Prunes
- Barley

- Bread
- Farro
- Popcorn
- Quinoa
- Unsweetened cereals
- Whole-grain cereals and crackers
- Broth-based soups
- Gelatin
- Nuts (any)
- Seeds (chia, flaxseeds, pumpkin, sunflower)
- Asparagus
- Brussels sprouts
- Carrots
- Collard greens
- Green beans
- Kale
- Lettuce
- Radishes
- Spinach
- Tomatoes
- Bulgur
- Pasta
- Pretzels
- Rice
- Wheat

**Other**

- Almond butter
- Lentils
- Peanut butter

**Vegetables**

- Broccoli
- Cabbage
- Cauliflower
- Corn
- Eggplant
- Kohlrabi
- Mushrooms
- Potatoes
- Sweet potatoes
- Wax beans

## Foods To Eat In Moderation

**Drinks**

- Wine
- Butter
- Margarine
- Wheat germ oil
- Crab
- Oysters

**Grains**

- Saltines and other crackers

**Others**

- Chocolate
- Chickpeas
- Chicken
- Lean cuts of red meat and pork (flank steak, ground, sirloin, tenderloin)

- 100% fruit juice

**Fats**

- Coconut oil
- Vegetable oil

**Fish/Seafood**

- Lobster
- Shrimp
- Oats and oatmeal
- Wheat bran
- Candy
- Fava beans

**Meats**

- Ham
- Turkey

## Foods To Avoid

**Dairy (Full-Fat)**

- Cream cheese
- Sour cream
- Whole milk
- Beer
- Fruit juices containing added sugar

**Fish/Seafood**

- Haddock
- Mackerel
- Perch

**Grains**

- Donuts and other pastries, full-fat ice cream
- Bacon
- Organ meats (brains, kidney, liver,

- Cheese
- Full-fat yogurt
- Premium ice cream

**Drinks**

- Drinks containing high-fructose corn syrup
- Liquor
- Anchovies
- Herring
- Mussels
- Sardines
- Sweetened cereal

**Meats**

- High-fat lunch meat (pickle loaf, roast beef)
- Processed meats (hot dogs, bacon,

- sweetbreads [thymus gland or pancreas])
- Lamb

**Others**

- Yeast extract (Marmite) and brewer's yeast (a nutritional supplement)

sausage)
- Wild game (duck, goose, venison)
- Mung beans

# Physical Activity

Exercise is vital for gout patients, but the activity must be moderate & gradual, not too strenuous. Moderate exercise is recommended for gout sufferers for 2 main reasons:

- To relieve stress and improve mood.
- To help maintain a healthy weight.

Physical activity recommended for gout sufferers:

- It would be best if you diversified & do some form of physical activity at least five days per week.
- Walk 30-60 minutes per day.

Fresh air is recommended—uses paths in remote areas and fields and avoids busy roads as much as possible. The atmosphere on the streets is saturated with pollutants emitted by vehicles.

In addition, moderate yoga is also recommended, integrated with deep breaths. It will help you strengthen your body and muscles & decrease stress.

**Physical activity to avoid**

It is not recommended gor gout sufferers to do strenuous physical activity such as running, lifting heavy weights, football, and the like. It is not just when the body digests food that purines are discharged from proteins; the body also breaks down proteins in large quantities during strenuous activity, and purines are released, which raises uric acid levels.

It's important to be mindful in training because sports injuries can trigger a gout attack.

# CHAPTER 1: Breakfast

## 1. Raspberry Oatmeal Bars

**Preparation time:** 5 minutes.
**Cooking time:** 15 minutes.
**Servings:** 6
**Ingredients:**

- 3 cups steel cut oats
- 3 large eggs
- 2 cups vanilla almond milk, unsweetened
- ⅓ cup erythritol
- 1 teaspoon pure vanilla extract
- ¼ teaspoon salt
- 1 cup frozen raspberries

**Directions:**
1. In a suitable bowl, mix together all the recipe ingredients except the berries. Fold in berries.
2. Layer a 6" cake pan with cooking oil. Transfer the prepared berry oat mixture to this pan and cover this pan with aluminum foil.
3. Pour 1 cup water into the instant pot and set the steam rack inside.
4. Place this pan with the oat mixture on top of the rack. Close the lid and secure it well.
5. Pressure cook for 15 minutes.
6. When done, release the pressure quickly until the float valve drops and then unlock lid.
7. Carefully remove this pan from your Instant pot and remove the foil.
8. Let it cool down before cutting into bars and serving.

**Per serving:** Calories: 236kcal; Fat: 5.2g; Carbs: 38.9g; Protein: 8.8g

## 2. Pistachio Smoothie

**Preparation time:** 5 minutes.
**Cooking time:** 0 minutes.
**Servings:** 2
**Ingredients:**

- 1 cup almond milk
- 1 cup shredded kale
- 2 frozen bananas
- ½ cup shelled pistachios
- 2 tablespoons pure maple syrup
- 1 teaspoon pure vanilla extract

**Directions:**
1. In a suitable blender, combine the milk, kale, bananas, pistachios, maple syrup, and vanilla. Blend until smooth and thick.

**Per serving:** Calories: 190kcal; Fat: 6.3g; Carbs: 30.2g; Protein: 4.5g

## 3. Broccoli Spinach Frittatas

**Preparation time:** 10 minutes.
**Cooking time:** 20 minutes.
**Servings:** 4
**Ingredients:**

- Olive oil, for greasing the muffin cups
- 8 eggs
- ¼ cup almond milk
- ½ teaspoon chopped fresh basil
- ½ cup chopped broccoli
- ½ cup shredded fresh spinach
- 1 scallion, white and green parts, chopped
- Pinch sea salt
- Pinch black pepper

**Directions:**
2. At 350 degrees F, preheat your oven.
3. Lightly oil a 6-cup muffin tin and keep it aside.
4. In a suitable bowl, whisk the eggs, almond milk, and basil until frothy.

5. Stir in the broccoli, spinach, and scallion. Spoon the prepared egg mixture into the muffin cups.
6. Bake for almost 20 minutes until the frittatas are puffed, golden, and cooked through.
7. Season with sea salt & black pepper and serve.

**Per serving:** Calories: 134kcal; Fat: 9g; Carbs: 2g; Protein: 11.6g

## 4. Turkey Hash

**Preparation time:** 10 minutes.
**Cooking time:** 26 minutes.
**Servings:** 4
**Ingredients:**

- 1½ pounds extra-lean ground turkey
- 1 sweet onion, chopped, or about 1 cup precut packaged onion
- 2 teaspoons bottled minced garlic
- 1 teaspoon ground ginger
- 2 pounds sweet potatoes, peeled, cooked, and diced
- Pinch sea salt
- Pinch black pepper, freshly ground
- Pinch ground cloves
- 1 cup chopped kale

**Directions:**

1. In a suitable skillet over medium-high heat, sauté the turkey for almost 10 minutes until it is cooked through.
2. Add the onion, garlic, and ginger. Sauté for almost 3 minutes.
3. Add the sweet potatoes, sea salt, pepper, and cloves. Reduce its heat to medium. Sauté for almost 10 minutes, while stirring until the sweet potato is heated through.
4. Stir in the kale. Cook for almost 3 minutes, while stirring until it has wilted.
5. Divide the hash among four bowls and serve.

**Per serving:** Calories: 356kcal; Fat: 8.4g; Carbs: 45.6g; Protein: 25.2g

## 5. Almond Granola

**Preparation time:** 5 minutes.
**Cooking time:** 7 minutes.
**Servings:** 8
**Ingredients:**

- 1½ cups old fashioned rolled oats
- ½ cup shredded coconut, unsweetened
- ¼ cup monk fruit sweetener
- ⅛ teaspoon salt
- ¾ cup almond butter
- ¼ cup coconut oil

**Directions:**

1. In a suitable bowl, mix together the oats, coconut, sweetener, and salt. Add the almond butter and oil and mix until well combined.
2. Layer a 6" cake pan with nonstick cooking oil. Transfer the oat mixture to this pan.
3. Add 1 cup water to your Instant pot. Set the steam rack inside, and place this pan on top of the steam rack. Close the lid and secure it well.
4. Pressure cook for 7 minutes.
5. When cooked, release the pressure quickly until the float valve drops and then unlock lid.
6. Remove this pan from your Instant pot and transfer the granola to your baking sheet to cool completely (at least 30 minutes) before serving.

**Per serving:** Calories: 192kcal; Fat: 16.3g; Carbs: 10.7g; Protein: 2.6g

### 6. Apple Cinnamon Oats

**Preparation time:** 10 minutes.
**Cooking time:** 4 minutes.
**Servings:** 6
**Ingredients:**

- 2 cups steel cut oats
- 3 cups vanilla almond milk, unsweetened
- 3 cups water
- 3 small apples, peeled, cored, and cut into 1"-thick chunks
- 2 teaspoons ground cinnamon
- ¼ cup date syrup
- ¼ teaspoon salt

**Directions:**

1. Add the steel cut oats, almond milk, water, apple chunks, cinnamon, date syrup, and salt to the instant pot then stir to combine. Close the lid and secure it well.
2. Pressure cook for 4 minutes.
3. When cooked, let pressure release naturally for almost 15 minutes, then quick-release any remaining pressure until float valve drops, then unlock lid.
4. Serve warm.

**Per serving:** Calories: 195kcal; Fat: 3.5g; Carbs: 38.5g; Protein: 4.5g

### 7. Sweet Potato Orange Smoothie

**Preparation time:** 5 minutes.
**Cooking time:** 0 minutes.
**Servings:** 2
**Ingredients:**

- ½ cup almond milk, unsweetened
- ½ cup orange juice, freshly squeezed
- 1 cup cooked sweet potato
- 1 banana
- 2 tablespoons pumpkin seeds
- 1 tablespoon pure maple syrup
- ½ teaspoon pure vanilla extract
- ½ teaspoon ground cinnamon
- 3 ice cubes

**Directions:**

1. In a suitable blender, combine the almond milk, orange juice, sweet potato, banana, pumpkin seeds, maple syrup, vanilla, and cinnamon. Blend until smooth.
2. Add the ice and blend until thick.

**Per serving:** Calories: 258kcal; Fat: 5.4g; Carbs: 50g; Protein: 5.5g

### 8. Banana Oatmeal

**Preparation time:** 5 minutes.
**Cooking time:** 7 minutes.
**Servings:** 6
**Ingredients:**

- 3 cups old fashioned rolled oats
- ¼ teaspoon salt
- 2 large bananas, mashed (1 heaping cup)
- 2 large eggs, lightly beaten
- ⅓ cup xylitol

**Directions:**

1. In a suitable bowl, set the oats, salt, bananas, eggs, and xylitol and stir to combine well.
2. Lightly Layer a 6" cake pan with cooking spray. Transfer the oat mixture to this pan.
3. Pour 1½ cups water into the inner pot. Place a steam rack in your Instant pot and place this pan on the steam rack. Close the lid and secure it well.
4. Pressure cook for 7 minutes.
5. When done, release the pressure quickly until the float valve drops and then unlock lid.
6. Allow the oatmeal to cool 5 minutes before serving.

**Per serving:** Calories: 139kcal; Fat: 3.1g; Carbs: 24g; Protein: 5.2g

## 9. Orange Oatmeal Muffins

**Preparation time:** 7 minutes.
**Cooking time:** 15 minutes.
**Servings:** 6
**Ingredients:**

- 3 cups old fashioned rolled oats
- 1 teaspoon baking powder
- ¼ teaspoon salt
- 1 teaspoon ground cinnamon
- ¼ cup vanilla almond milk, unsweetened
- ¼ cup fresh orange juice
- 3⅓ cups mashed bananas
- 1 large egg
- ¼ cup erythritol

**Directions:**

1. In a suitable bowl, mix all of the ingredients together, while stirring until well combined.
2. Place six silicone muffin cups inside of a 6" cake pan. Spoon the oatmeal mixture into your muffin cups. Cover this pan with aluminum foil.
3. Pour 1 cup water into your Instant Pot and set the steam rack inside. Set the cake pan with the muffins on the rack. Close the lid and secure it well.
4. Pressure cook for 15 minutes.
5. When cooked, release the pressure quickly until the float valve drops and then unlock lid.
6. Carefully remove this pan from your Instant pot and remove the foil from the top. Let the muffins cool 15 minutes before eating. They will become firmer as they cool.

**Per serving:** Calories: 148kcal; Fat: 2.5g; Carbs: 29g; Protein: 4.5g

## 10. Coconut Strawberry Porridge

**Preparation time:** 5 minutes.
**Cooking time:** 0 minutes.
**Servings:** 4
**Ingredients:**

- ¾ cup water
- ¾ cup almond milk, unsweetened
- 1 teaspoon pure vanilla extract
- ¼ cup chia seeds
- ¼ cup shredded coconut, unsweetened
- 2 tablespoons raw honey
- ½ cup sliced fresh strawberries

**Directions:**

1. In a suitable bowl, whisk the water, almond milk, and vanilla until well blended.
2. Stir in the chia seeds, cover the bowl, and refrigerate it for a minimum of 30 minutes and up to overnight.
3. Stir the coconut and honey into the chilled porridge. Spoon the porridge into four bowls.
4. Serve topped with the strawberries.

**Per serving:** Calories: 173kcal; Fat: 11g; Carbs: 17g; Protein: 2.8g

## 11. Banana Coconut Pancakes

**Preparation time:** 10 minutes.
**Cooking time:** 10 minutes.
**Servings:** 4
**Ingredients:**

- ½ cup almond flour
- ¼ cup coconut flour
- 1 teaspoon baking soda
- 3 eggs, beaten
- 2 bananas, mashed
- 1 teaspoon pure vanilla extract
- 1 tablespoon coconut oil
- Pure maple syrup, for serving
- Fresh fruit, for serving

**Directions:**
1. In a suitable bowl, stir together the almond flour, coconut flour, and baking soda until well mixed.
2. Make a small well at the center of it and add the eggs, bananas, and vanilla. Beat together until well blended.
3. Place a suitable skillet over medium-high heat and add the coconut oil.
4. For each pancake, pour ¼ cup of batter into this skillet, four per batch. Cook for almost 3 minutes until the bottom is golden and the bubbles on the surface burst. Flip and cook for almost 2 minutes more until golden and cooked through. Transfer to a plate and repeat with any remaining batter.
5. Serve.

**Per serving:** Calories: 213kcal; Fat: 10g; Carbs: 24.6g; Protein: 7.5g

## 12. Banana Date Porridge

**Preparation time:** 5 minutes.
**Cooking time:** 4 minutes.
**Servings:** 4
**Ingredients:**
- 1 cup buckwheat groats
- 1½ cups vanilla almond milk, unsweetened
- 1 cup water
- 1 large banana, mashed
- 5 pitted dates, chopped
- ¾ teaspoon ground cinnamon
- ¾ teaspoon pure vanilla extract

**Directions:**
1. Set the buckwheat groats, almond milk, water, banana, dates, cinnamon, and vanilla in your Instant pot and stir. Close the lid and secure it well.
2. Pressure cook for 4 minutes.
3. When done, release the pressure quickly until the float valve drops and then unlock lid.
4. Allow the porridge to cool slightly before spooning into bowls to serve.

**Per serving:** Calories: 178kcal; Fat: 2.2g; Carbs: 37.9g; Protein: 4.8g

## 13. Apple-Cinnamon Smoothie

**Preparation time:** 5 minutes.
**Cooking time:** 0 minutes.
**Servings:** 2
**Ingredients:**
- 1 cup canned lite coconut milk
- 1 apple, cored and cut into chunks
- 1 banana
- ¼ cup almond butter
- 1 tablespoon raw honey
- ½ teaspoon ground cinnamon
- 4 ice cubes

**Directions:**
1. In a suitable blender, combine the coconut milk, apple, banana, almond butter, honey, and cinnamon. Blend until smooth.
2. Add the ice and blend until thick.

**Per serving:** Calories: 224kcal; Fat: 7.5g; Carbs: 42.9g; Protein: 2.9g

## 14. Fruity Breakfast Bars

**Preparation time:** 15 minutes.
**Cooking time:** 30 minutes.
**Servings:** 6
**Ingredients:**
- ½ cup pitted dates
- ¾ cup toasted sunflower seeds
- ¾ cup toasted pumpkin seeds
- ¾ cup white sesame seeds
- ½ cup dried blueberries
- ½ cup dried cherries
- ¼ cup flaxseed

- ½ cup almond butter

**Directions:**
1. At 325 degrees F, preheat your oven.
2. Layer an 8-by-8-inch baking dish with parchment paper.
3. In a suitable food processor, blend the dates until chopped into a paste.
4. Add the sunflower seeds, pumpkin seeds, sesame seeds, blueberries, cherries, and flaxseed, and pulse to combine. Scoop the prepared mixture into a suitable bowl.
5. Stir in the almond butter. Transfer the prepared mixture to the prepared dish and press it down firmly.
6. Bake for almost 30 minutes until firm and golden brown.
7. Cool for almost 1 hour, until it is at room temperature. Remove from the baking dish and cut into 12 squares.
8. Refrigerate in any sealed container for up to 1 week.

**Per serving:** Calories: 242kcal; Fat: 13.2g; Carbs: 26.7g; Protein: 7g

## 15. Artichoke Egg Casserole

**Preparation time:** 10 minutes.
**Cooking time:** 18 minutes.
**Servings:** 8
**Ingredients:**
- 12 large eggs
- ¼ cup water
- 4 cups baby spinach, chopped
- 1 (14-ounce) can baby artichoke hearts, drained and chopped
- 1 tablespoon chopped fresh chives
- 1 tablespoon fresh lemon juice
- ¾ teaspoon table salt
- ½ teaspoon black pepper
- ¼ teaspoon garlic salt

**Directions:**
1. Layer a 6" round pan or 7-cup round glass bowl with cooking spray.
2. In a suitable bowl, whisk together the eggs and water.
3. Stir in the spinach, artichokes, chives, lemon juice, table salt, pepper, and garlic salt.
4. Transfer the prepared mixture to the prepared pan.
5. Place 2 cups water in your Instant pot and set the steam rack inside. Place this pan on top of the steam rack. Close the lid and secure it well.
6. Pressure cook for 18 minutes.
7. When done, release the pressure quickly until the float valve drops and then unlock lid.
8. Remove egg casserole from pot and allow to cool 5 minutes before slicing and serving.

**Per serving:** Calories: 112kcal; Fat: 7.5g; Carbs: 1.3g; Protein: 9.9g

## 16. Coconut Chocolate Oatmeal

**Preparation time:** 5 minutes.
**Cooking time:** 6 minutes approximately.
**Servings:** 4
**Ingredients:**
- 1 cup steel cut oats
- 1 (13.25-ounce) can full-fat coconut milk, unsweetened
- 2 cups water
- ½ cup cacao powder
- ½ cup erythritol
- ⅛ teaspoon sea salt

**Directions:**
1. Set the oats, coconut milk, water, cacao powder, erythritol, and salt in your Instant pot and stir to combine. Close the lid and secure it well.
2. Pressure cook for 6 minutes approximately.

3. When cooked, release the pressure quickly until the float valve drops and then unlock lid.
  4. Allow the oatmeal to cool slightly before spooning into bowls to serve.

**Per serving:** Calories: 280kcal; Fat: 14.7g; Carbs: 30.6g; Protein: 6.8g

## 17. Poppy Oatmeal Cups

**Preparation time:** 5 minutes.
**Cooking time:** 5 minutes.
**Servings:** 4
**Ingredients:**

- 2 cups old fashioned rolled oats
- 1 teaspoon baking powder
- 2 tablespoons erythritol
- 1 tablespoon poppy seeds
- ¼ teaspoon salt
- 1 large egg
- Juice and zest from 1 Meyer lemon
- 1 cup vanilla almond milk, unsweetened

**Directions:**

1. Lightly grease four (8-ounce) ramekin dishes. Set aside.
2. In a suitable bowl, mix together the oats, baking powder, erythritol, poppy seeds, and salt. Add the egg, juice and zest from the lemon, and the almond milk and stir to combine. Divide the oatmeal mixture into the four dishes.
3. Pour ½ cup water into your Instant Pot. Set the steam rack inside your Instant pot and set the ramekins on top of the rack. Close the lid and secure it well.
4. Pressure cook for 5 minutes.
5. When cooked, release the pressure quickly until the float valve drops and then unlock lid.
6. The ramekins will be hot when you open the lid, so be sure to use your mini oven mitts to lift them out of the instant pot and let them cool before serving.

**Per serving:** Calories: 212kcal; Fat: 7.1g; Carbs: 29.4g; Protein: 9.2g

## 18. Pumpkin Porridge

**Preparation time:** 2 minutes.
**Cooking time:** 1 minute
**Servings:** 4
**Ingredients:**

- ¾ cup dry quinoa
- 2 cups water
- ¾ cup pumpkin purée
- ¼ cup monk fruit sweetener
- 1½ teaspoons pumpkin pie spice
- 1 teaspoon pure vanilla extract
- ¼ teaspoon salt

**Directions:**

1. Using a fine-mesh strainer, rinse the quinoa very well until the water runs clear.
2. Add the quinoa, water, pumpkin purée, sweetener, pumpkin pie spice, vanilla, and salt to the inner pot. Stir to combine. Close the lid and secure it well.
3. Pressure cook for 1 minute.
4. When cooked, release the pressure quickly until the float valve drops and then unlock lid.
5. Allow the quinoa to cool slightly before spooning into bowls to serve.

**Per serving:** Calories: 144kcal; Fat: 2.4g; Carbs: 25.9g; Protein: 5.1g

## 19. Blueberry Quinoa Porridge

**Preparation time:** 2 minutes.
**Cooking time:** 1 minute
**Servings:** 6
**Ingredients:**

- 1½ cups dry quinoa

- 3 cups water
- 1 cup frozen wild blueberries
- ½ teaspoon pure stevia powder
- 1 teaspoon pure vanilla extract

**Directions:**
1. Using a fine-mesh strainer, rinse the quinoa very well until the water runs clear.
2. Add the quinoa, water, blueberries, stevia, and vanilla to the inner pot. Stir to combine. Close the lid and secure it well.
3. Pressure cook for 1 minute.
4. When cooked, release the pressure quickly until the float valve drops and then unlock lid.
5. Allow the quinoa to cool slightly before spooning into bowls to serve.

**Per serving:** Calories: 311kcal; Fat: 2.7g; Carbs: 64.7g; Protein: 6.3g

## 20. Sweet Potato Casserole

**Preparation time:** 15 minutes.
**Cooking time:** 30 minutes.
**Servings:** 4
**Ingredients:**

- Olive oil, for greasing the baking dish
- 1 cup diced cooked sweet potato
- 1 cup chopped blanched cauliflower
- 1 cup shredded kale
- 1 scallion, white and green parts, chopped
- 1 teaspoon chopped fresh basil
- 8 eggs
- ¼ cup almond milk, unsweetened
- 1 teaspoon ground cumin
- 1 teaspoon ground coriander
- Pinch sea salt
- Pinch black pepper, freshly ground

**Directions:**
1. At 375 degrees F, preheat your oven.
2. Lightly layer a 9-by-13-inch baking dish with olive oil.
3. Evenly spread the sweet potato, cauliflower, kale, scallion, and basil in the prepared dish.
4. In a suitable bowl, whisk the eggs, almond milk, cumin, coriander, sea salt, and pepper. Pour the prepared egg mixture into the baking dish, lightly tapping the dish on the counter to distribute the eggs among the vegetables.
5. Bake for almost 30 minutes until the eggs are set and the top is lightly golden.

**Per serving:** Calories: 191kcal; Fat: 9.2g; Carbs: 14.8g; Protein: 13.3g

## 21. Raspberry Pineapple Smoothie

**Preparation time:** 5 minutes.
**Cooking time:** 0 minutes.
**Servings:** 2
**Ingredients:**

- 1 cup coconut water
- ½ cup pineapple juice, unsweetened
- 1 banana
- ½ cup fresh raspberries
- ½ cup shredded coconut
- 3 ice cubes

**Directions:**
1. In a suitable blender, combine the pineapple juice, coconut water, banana, raspberries, and coconut. Blend until smooth.
2. Add the ice and blend until thick.

**Per serving:** Calories: 263kcal; Fat: 16.5g; Carbs: 25.8g; Protein: 3.4g

## 22. Beef Breakfast

**Preparation time:** 20 minutes.
**Cooking time:** 20 minutes.

**Servings:** 4
**Ingredients:**
- 1 tablespoon olive oil
- 1 pound lean ground beef
- 2 teaspoons bottled minced garlic
- 2 cups chopped cauliflower
- 1 cup diced carrots
- 1 zucchini, diced
- 2 scallions, white and green parts, chopped
- Sea salt
- Black pepper
- 2 tablespoons chopped fresh parsley

**Directions:**
1. Place a suitable skillet over medium-high heat and add the olive oil.
2. Add the ground beef and garlic. Sauté for almost 8 minutes until cooked through.
3. Stir in the cauliflower, carrots, and zucchini. Sauté for almost 10 minutes until tender.
4. Stir in the scallions and sauté for almost 1 minute more.
5. Season the prepared mixture with black pepper and sea salt. Serve topped with the parsley.

**Per serving:** Calories: 277kcal; Fat: 10.7g; Carbs: 8g; Protein: 36.4g

### 23. Triple Berry Oats

**Preparation time:** 5 minutes.
**Cooking time:** 4 minutes.
**Servings:** 6
**Ingredients:**
- 2 cups steel cut oats
- 3 cups almond milk, unsweetened
- 3 cups water
- 1 teaspoon pure vanilla extract
- ⅓ cup monk fruit sweetener
- ¼ teaspoon salt
- 1½ cups frozen berry blend with strawberries, blackberries, and raspberries

**Directions:**
1. Add the steel cut oats, almond milk, water, vanilla, sweetener, and salt to the instant pot and stir to combine. Set the frozen berries on top. Close the lid and secure it well.
2. Pressure cook for 4 minutes.
3. When done, let pressure release naturally for almost 15 minutes, then quick-release any remaining pressure until float valve drops, then unlock lid. Serve warm.

**Per serving:** Calories: 125kcal; Fat: 3.5g; Carbs: 19.6g; Protein: 4.1g

### 24. Pancake Bites

**Preparation time:** 10 minutes.
**Cooking time:** 6 minutes approximately.
**Servings:** 3
**Ingredients:**
- 1¾ cups old fashioned rolled oats
- 3 small ripe bananas
- 3 large eggs
- 2 tablespoons erythritol
- 1 teaspoon ground cinnamon
- 1 teaspoon pure vanilla extract
- 1 teaspoon baking powder

**Directions:**
1. Set the oats, bananas, eggs, erythritol, cinnamon, vanilla, and baking powder in a large, powerful blender and blend 'til very smooth, about 1 minute.
2. Pour the prepared mixture into a silicone mold with seven wells. Place a paper towel on top and then top with aluminum foil. Tighten the edges to prevent extra moisture getting inside.

Set the mold on top of your steam rack with handles.
3. Pour 1 cup water into the inner pot. Set the steam rack and mold inside. Close the lid and secure it well.
4. Pressure cook for 6 minutes approximately.
5. When cooked, release the pressure quickly until the float valve drops and then unlock lid.
6. Pull the steam rack and mold out of the instant pot and remove the aluminum foil and paper towel. Allow this pancake bites to cool completely, and then use a knife to pull the edges of the bites away from the mold. Press on the bottom of the mold and this pancake bites will pop right out.

**Per serving:** Calories: 331kcal; Fat: 8.2g; Carbs: 54.3g; Protein: 13.1g

## 25. Tofu Scramble

**Preparation time:** 10 minutes
**Cooking time:** 8 minutes
**Servings:** 4
**Ingredients:**

- 3 tablespoons extra-virgin olive oil
- 3 green onions, sliced
- 3 garlic cloves, peeled and sliced
- 1 15-oz package firm tofu, drained and diced
- Kosher salt, to taste
- 1 cup mung bean sprouts
- 2 tablespoons mint, chopped
- 2 tablespoons parsley, chopped
- 1 tablespoon lime juice
- Fish sauce for serving
- Cooked brown rice for serving

**Directions:**
1. Mix olive oil, white parts of the green onions, and garlic in a cold sauté pan. Turn the heat to low. As the aromatics warm, stirring occasionally for 4 minutes almost.
2. Add the tofu and salt and reduce its heat to medium. Cook, occasionally stirring, until the tofu is well coated with the oil and warmed for 3 minutes almost.
3. Add mung bean sprouts and cook for 1 minute.
4. Stir in the green parts of the green onions and the mint, parsley, and lime juice. Stir to combine. Taste, adding fish sauce or additional lime juice, if desired.
5. Serve the scramble on its own or over brown rice with poached eggs on top.

**Per serving:** Calories: 185kcal; Fat: 14.9g; Carbs: 5.6g; Protein: 11.1g

## 26. Spicy Quinoa

**Preparation time:** 10 minutes
**Cooking time:** 20 minutes
**Servings:** 4
**Ingredients:**

- 1 cup quinoa, rinsed
- 2 cups water
- ½ cup shredded coconut
- ¼ cup hemp seeds
- 2 tablespoons flaxseed
- 1 teaspoon ground cinnamon
- 1 teaspoon vanilla extract
- 1 pinch salt
- 1 cup fresh berries of your choice
- ¼ cup chopped hazelnuts

**Directions:**
1. In a suitable saucepan over high heat, combine the quinoa and water.
2. Bring to a boil, reduce its heat to a simmer, and cook for 15 to 20 minutes, or 'til the quinoa is cooked through.

3. Stir in the coconut, hemp seeds, flaxseed, cinnamon, vanilla, and salt.
4. Divide the cooked quinoa among four bowls and top each serving with ¼ cup of berries and 1 tablespoon of hazelnuts.

**Per serving:** Calories: 264kcal; Fat: 10g; Carbs: 35.4g; Protein: 8g

## 27. Black Bean Breakfast

**Preparation time:** 35 minutes
**Cooking time:** 5-10 minutes
**Servings:** 4
**Ingredients:**
Pico de Gallo:

- 2 cups cherry tomatoes, halved
- 1 jalapeño, minced
- 2 tablespoons chopped cilantro
- 2 tablespoons diced white onion
- 1 tablespoon lime juice
- Kosher salt

Avocado Mash:

- 2 avocados
- Kosher salt
- 1 tablespoon diced white onion
- 1 tablespoon lime juice
- 1 to 2 dashes of hot sauce
- 1 (15-oz) can black beans, rinsed & drained
- 1 tablespoon lime juice
- Kosher salt
- 4 eggs, poached or scrambled
- Hot sauce for serving

**Directions:**
1. For the Pico de Gallo: Combine the jalapeño, tomatoes, cilantro, onion, and lime juice in a suitable bowl. Taste, add salt if desired, and stir to mix.
2. To make the avocado mash: place the avocados in a suitable bowl or molcajete with a generous sprinkling of salt. Using a fork or pastry blender, mash until the avocados are a bit chunky or completely smooth, depending on your preference. Stir in the onion, lime juice, and hot sauce. Taste, adding more salt or more hot sauce if needed.
3. In a suitable saucepan, warm the black beans and lime juice, mash gently with a fork, and season with salt.
4. Place one-fourth of the black beans in each bowl, then one-fourth of the avocado mash. Top with an egg, then the Pico de Gallo and a dash of hot sauce. Serve immediately.

**Per serving:** Calories: 455kcal; Fat: 24.9g; Carbs: 44.3g; Protein: 18.9g

## 28. Tomatoes Egg Scramble

**Preparation time:** 5 minutes
**Cooking time:** 10 minutes
**Servings:** 2
**Ingredients:**

- 4 eggs
- 2 teaspoons chopped fresh oregano
- 1 tablespoon extra-virgin olive oil
- 1 cup cherry tomatoes, halved
- ½ garlic clove, sliced
- ½ avocado, sliced

**Directions:**
1. In a suitable bowl, beat the eggs until well combined; whisk in the oregano.
2. Place a suitable skillet over medium heat. Once your pan is hot, add the olive oil.
3. Pour the eggs into the skillet and use either a heat-resistant spatula or wooden spoon to scramble the eggs. Transfer the eggs to a serving dish.

4. Add the cherry tomatoes and garlic to the pan and sauté for almost 2 minutes. Spoon the tomatoes over the eggs and top the dish with the avocado slices.

**Per serving:** Calories: 310kcal; Fat: 25.9g; Carbs: 9.7g; Protein: 13g

## 29. Coconut Pancakes

**Preparation time:** 10 minutes
**Cooking time:** 20 minutes
**Servings:** 4
**Ingredients:**

- 4 eggs
- 1 cup coconut milk
- 1 tablespoon melted coconut oil
- 1 tablespoon maple syrup
- 1 teaspoon vanilla extract
- ½ cup coconut flour
- 1 teaspoon baking soda

½ teaspoon salt

**Directions:**

1. In a suitable bowl, mix together the eggs, coconut milk, coconut oil, maple syrup, and vanilla with an electric mixer.
2. In a suitable bowl, stir together the coconut flour, baking soda, and salt. Add the dry ingredients to your wet ingredients and beat well until smooth and lump-free.
3. Lightly grease a suitable skillet with coconut oil. Place it over medium-high heat.
4. Add the batter in ½-cup scoops and cook for almost 3 minutes, or until golden brown on the bottom. Flip and cook for almost 2 minutes more.
5. Stack the pancakes on a plate while continuing to cook the remaining batter. This makes about 8 pancakes.

**Per serving:** Calories: 180kcal; Fat: 10.3g; Carbs: 14.6g; Protein: 7.8g

## 30. Overnight Muesli

**Preparation time:** 10 minutes
**Cooking time:** 0 minutes
**Servings:** 4 to 6
**Ingredients:**

- 2 cups gluten-free rolled oats
- 1¾ cups coconut milk
- ¼ cup sugar-free apple juice
- 1 tablespoon apple cider vinegar
- 1 apple, cored and chopped
- Dash ground cinnamon

**Directions:**

1. In a suitable bowl, stir together the oats, coconut milk, apple juice, and vinegar.
2. Cover and refrigerate overnight.
3. The next morning, stir in the chopped apple and season the muesli with the cinnamon.

**Per serving:** Calories: 384kcal; Fat: 32.2g; Carbs: 24.2g; Protein: 5.4g

# CHAPTER 2: Vegetarian

## 31. Boiled Beans

**Preparation time:** 10 minutes.
**Cooking time:** 8 hours
**Servings:** 6
**Ingredients:**

- 1 pound dried beans, any kind
- Water

**Directions:**

1. Rinse the beans, then pick out any broken ones or possible rocks or dirt particles.
2. Put the beans in a suitable bowl or in your slow cooker and cover with water. Let it soak for a minimum of 8 hours, or overnight.

3. Drain and rinse the beans well. Put them in your slow cooker and cover with 2 inches of fresh water.
4. Cover your slow cooker with its lid. Slow cook for 8 hours until soft and cooked through. Drain and serve.

**Per serving:** Calories: 140kcal; Fat: 5g; Carbs: 23g; Protein: 8g

### 32. Quinoa With Pepperoncini

**Preparation time:** 15 minutes.
**Cooking time:** 8 hours.
**Servings:** 4 to 6
**Ingredients:**

- 1½ cups quinoa, rinsed well
- 3 cups vegetable broth
- ½ teaspoon sea salt
- ½ teaspoon garlic powder
- ¼ teaspoon dried oregano
- ¼ teaspoon dried basil leaves
- Black pepper
- 3 cups arugula
- ½ cup diced tomatoes
- ⅓ cup sliced pepperoncini
- ¼ cup lemon juice
- 3 tablespoons olive oil

**Directions:**
1. In your slow cooker, combine the quinoa, broth, salt, garlic powder, oregano, and basil, and season with pepper.
2. Cover the cooker then set to low. Cook for almost 6 to 8 hours.
3. In a suitable bowl, toss together the arugula, tomatoes, pepperoncini, lemon juice, and olive oil.
4. When the quinoa is done, add it to the arugula salad, mix well, and serve.

**Per serving:** Calories: 245kcal; Fat: 10.5g; Carbs: 29.2g; Protein: 8.9g

### 33. Minestrone Soup

**Preparation time:** 15 minutes.
**Cooking time:** 8 hours.
**Servings:** 4
**Ingredients:**

- 1 (14-ounce) can diced tomatoes with their juice
- 1 (14-ounce) can kidney beans, drained and rinsed well
- 2 celery stalks, diced
- 2 carrots, diced
- 1 zucchini, diced
- 1 small onion, diced
- 1 tablespoon lemon juice
- 1 teaspoon sea salt
- ½ teaspoon garlic powder
- ½ teaspoon dried oregano
- ½ teaspoon dried basil leaves
- ½ teaspoon dried rosemary
- 2 bay leaves
- 6 cups vegetable broth
- 1 cup packed fresh spinach

**Directions:**
1. In your slow cooker, combine the tomatoes, kidney beans, celery, carrots, zucchini, onion, lemon juice, salt, garlic powder, oregano, basil, rosemary, bay leaves, and broth.
2. Cover the cooker then set to low. Cook for almost 6 to 8 hours.
3. Remove and discard the bay leaves. Stir in the spinach and let wilt (about 5 minutes) before serving.

**Per serving:** Calories: 298kcal; Fat: 2.2g; Carbs: 49.9g; Protein: 21.3g

### 34. Basic Quinoa

**Preparation time:** 15 minutes.
**Cooking time:** 6 hours.
**Servings:** 4
**Ingredients:**

- 2 cups quinoa, rinsed well
- 4 cups vegetable broth

**Directions:**
1. In your slow cooker, combine the quinoa and broth.
2. Cover the cooker then set to low. Cook for almost 4 to 6 hours. Fluff with a fork, cool, and serve.

**Per serving:** Calories: 234kcal; Fat: 4.3g; Carbs: 37g; Protein: 11.2g

## 35. Baked Spiced Tofu

**Preparation time:** 5 minutes.
**Cooking time:** 20 minutes.
**Servings:** 4
**Ingredients:**

- 2 teaspoons ground cumin
- 2 teaspoons smoked paprika
- 1 teaspoon ground cinnamon
- 1 teaspoon garlic powder
- 1 teaspoon ground turmeric
- 1 teaspoon red pepper flakes
- 1 teaspoon salt
- 1 (14-ounce) package extra-firm tofu, drained
- ⅓ cup extra-virgin olive oil
- 2 tablespoons tahini or unsweetened almond butter

**Directions:**
1. At 400 degrees F, preheat your oven and layer a baking sheet with parchment paper.
2. In a suitable bowl, combine the cumin, paprika, cinnamon, garlic powder, turmeric, red pepper flakes, and salt. Place half of the spice mixture in a suitable bowl, reserving the other half.
3. Cut the tofu block into four large rectangles and place on several layers of paper towels. Cover with additional paper towels then press down to release the water. Cut the rectangles into 1-inch cubes and transfer to the bowl with the spice mixture. Toss to coat well.
4. Arrange the tofu cubes ½ inch apart in a single layer on the prepared baking sheet, reserving the bowl. Bake the tofu for almost 15 to 20 minutes, until it is crispy and golden.
5. While the tofu bakes, add the olive oil and tahini to the reserved spice mixture and whisk until smooth.
6. In the large reserved bowl, combine the baked tofu with the oil-tahini mixture and toss well to coat. Let it cool down if not serving warm.
7. Transfer to a storage container, cover and allow to marinate 24 hours refrigerated.

**Per serving:** Calories: 293kcal; Fat: 27.1g; Carbs: 6.2g; Protein: 11.7g

## 36. Spiced Sweet Potato Soup

**Preparation time:** 15 minutes.
**Cooking time:** 8 hours.
**Servings:** 4
**Ingredients:**

- 4 cups vegetable broth, more if needed
- 1 (15-ounce) can diced tomatoes
- 2 medium sweet potatoes, peeled and diced
- 1 medium onion, diced
- 1 jalapeño pepper, seeded and diced
- ½ cup unsalted almond butter
- ½ teaspoon sea salt
- ½ teaspoon garlic powder
- ½ teaspoon ground turmeric
- ½ teaspoon ground ginger
- ¼ teaspoon ground cinnamon
- Pinch ground nutmeg
- ½ cup full-fat coconut milk

**Directions:**
1. In your slow cooker, combine the broth, tomatoes, sweet potatoes, onion, jalapeño, almond butter, salt, garlic powder, turmeric, ginger, cinnamon, and nutmeg.
2. Cover the cooker then set to low. Cook for almost 6 to 8 hours.
3. Stir in the coconut milk after cooking.
4. Using an immersion blender, purée the soup until smooth and serve.

**Per serving:** Calories: 272kcal; Fat: 17.3g; Carbs: 24.3g; Protein: 8.6g

## 37. Coconutty Brown Rice

**Preparation time:** 15 minutes.
**Cooking time:** 3 hours.
**Servings:** 4 to 6
**Ingredients:**

- 2 cups brown rice, soaked in water overnight, drained, and rinsed
- 3 cups water
- 1½ cups full-fat coconut milk
- 1 teaspoon sea salt
- ½ teaspoon ground ginger
- Black pepper

**Directions:**
1. In your slow cooker, combine the rice, water, coconut milk, salt, and ginger. Season with pepper and stir to incorporate the spices.
2. Cover the cooker then set to high. Cook for almost 3 hours and serve.

**Per serving:** Calories: 230kcal; Fat: 1.7g; Carbs: 48.4g; Protein: 4.8g

## 38. Thai Vegetable Soup

**Preparation time:** 5 minutes.
**Cooking time:** 0 minutes.
**Servings:** 4 to 6
**Ingredients:**

- 4 cups vegetable broth
- ½ cup sliced mushrooms
- 3 carrots, diced
- 1 bunch baby bok choy
- 1 sweet potato, peeled and diced
- 1 small head broccoli, florets chopped
- 1 small onion, diced
- 1 lemongrass stalk, chopped into 1-inch segments
- 1 tablespoon lime juice
- 1 tablespoon curry paste
- 2 teaspoons fish sauce
- ¾ teaspoon sea salt
- ½ teaspoon ground ginger
- ½ teaspoon garlic powder
- ¾ cup full-fat coconut milk
- Fresh cilantro leaves, for garnishing

**Directions:**
1. In your slow cooker, stir together the broth, mushrooms, carrots, bok choy, sweet potato, broccoli, onion, lemongrass, lime juice, curry paste, fish sauce, salt, ginger, and garlic powder.
2. Cover the cooker then set to low. Cook for almost 6 to 8 hours.
3. Stir in the coconut milk and garnish with the cilantro before serving.

**Per serving:** Calories: 138kcal; Fat: 3.8g; Carbs: 18.6g; Protein: 7.9g

## 39. Butter Chickpeas

**Preparation time:** 15 minutes.
**Cooking time:** 8 hours.
**Servings:** 4
**Ingredients:**

- 1 tablespoon coconut oil
- 1 medium onion, diced
- 1 pound dried chickpeas, soaked in water overnight, drained, and rinsed
- 2 cups full-fat coconut milk

- 1 (15-ounce) can crushed tomatoes
- 2 tablespoons almond butter
- 2 tablespoons curry powder
- 1½ teaspoons garlic powder
- 1 teaspoon ground ginger
- ½ teaspoon sea salt
- ½ teaspoon ground cumin
- ½ teaspoon chili powder

**Directions:**
1. Layer the slow cooker with coconut oil.
2. Layer the onion along the bottom of your slow cooker.
3. Add the chickpeas, coconut milk, tomatoes, almond butter, curry powder, garlic powder, ginger, salt, cumin, and chili powder. Gently stir to ensure the spices are mixed into the liquid.
4. Cover the cooker and set to low. Cook for almost 6 to 8 hours, until the chickpeas are soft, and serve.

**Per serving:** Calories: 478kcal; Fat: 19.6g; Carbs: 59.9g; Protein: 18.4g

### 40. Wild Rice Mushroom Soup

**Preparation time:** 15 minutes.
**Cooking time:** 8 hours.
**Servings:** 4
**Ingredients:**

- 1½ cups uncooked wild rice
- 6 cups vegetable broth
- 2 carrots, diced
- 1 celery stalk, diced
- ½ medium onion, diced
- ¼ cup dried porcini mushrooms
- 1 tablespoon extra-virgin olive oil
- 1 teaspoon sea salt
- ½ teaspoon garlic powder
- ½ teaspoon dried thyme leaves
- 1 bay leaf
- Black pepper

**Directions:**
1. In your slow cooker, combine the rice, broth, carrots, celery, onion, mushrooms, olive oil, salt, garlic powder, thyme, and bay leaf, and season with pepper.
2. Cover the cooker then set to low. Cook for almost 6 to 8 hours.
3. Remove and discard the bay leaf before serving.

**Per serving:** Calories: 240kcal; Fat: 4.2g; Carbs: 37.4g; Protein: 12.8g

### 41. Sweet Potato Leek Soup

**Preparation time:** 15 minutes.
**Cooking time:** 5 hrs.
**Servings:** 4 to 6
**Ingredients:**

- 5 medium sweet potatoes, peeled and chopped
- 1 leek, washed and sliced
- 1½ teaspoons garlic powder
- 1 teaspoon sea salt
- ½ teaspoon ground turmeric
- ¼ teaspoon ground cumin
- 4 cups vegetable broth
- Black pepper

**Directions:**
1. In your slow cooker, combine the sweet potatoes, leek, garlic powder, salt, turmeric, cumin, and broth, and season with pepper.
2. Cover the cooker then set to low. Cook for almost 4 to 5 hours.
3. Using an immersion blender, purée the soup until smooth and serve.

**Per serving:** Calories: 192kcal; Fat: 1.2g; Carbs: 39.6g; Protein: 5.8g

### 42. Spaghetti Squash

**Preparation time:** 15 minutes.

**Cooking time:** 8 hours.
**Servings:** 4 to 6
**Ingredients:**

- 1 spaghetti squash, washed well
- 2 cups water

**Directions:**

1. Using a fork, poke 10 to 15 holes all around the outside of the spaghetti squash. Put the squash and the water in your slow cooker.
2. Cover the cooker then set to low. Cook for 8 hours.
3. Transfer the squash from the slow cooker to a cutting board. Let sit for almost 15 minutes to cool.
4. Halve the squash lengthwise. Using a spoon, scrape the seeds out of the center of the squash. Then, using your fork, scrape at the flesh until it shreds into a spaghetti-like texture. Serve warm.

**Per serving:** Calories: 26kcal; Fat: 0.3g; Carbs: 5.4g; Protein: 2g

### 43. Baked Navy Beans

**Preparation time:** 15 minutes.
**Cooking time:** 8 hours
**Servings:** 4 to 6
**Ingredients:**

- 2 cups dried navy beans, soaked in water overnight, drained, and rinsed
- 6 cups vegetable broth
- ¼ cup dried cranberries
- 1 medium sweet onion, diced
- ½ cup sugar-free ketchup
- 3 tablespoons olive oil
- 2 tablespoons maple syrup
- 2 tablespoons molasses
- 1 tablespoon apple cider vinegar
- 1 teaspoon Dijon mustard
- 1 teaspoon sea salt
- ½ teaspoon garlic powder

**Directions:**

1. In your slow cooker, combine the beans, broth, cranberries, onion, ketchup, olive oil, maple syrup, molasses, vinegar, mustard, salt, and garlic powder.
2. Cover the cooker then set to low. Cook for 7 to 8 hours and serve.

**Per serving:** Calories: 380kcal; Fat: 9.5g; Carbs: 54.8g; Protein: 20.6g

### 44. Cauliflower Rice Risotto

**Preparation time:** 15 minutes.
**Cooking time:** 5 hours.
**Servings:** 4
**Ingredients:**

- 1 pound riced cauliflower
- 1 celery stalk, minced
- 1 small shallot, minced
- ¼ cup vegetable broth
- ½ teaspoon garlic powder
- ½ teaspoon sea salt
- Black pepper

**Directions:**

1. In your slow cooker, combine the riced cauliflower, celery, shallot, broth, garlic powder, and salt, and season with pepper. Stir well.
2. Cover the cooker then set to low. Cook for almost 4 to 5 hours and serve.

**Per serving:** Calories: 27kcal; Fat: 0.2g; Carbs: 4.2g; Protein: 1.9g

### 45. Harvest Rice

**Preparation time:** 15 minutes.
**Cooking time:** 3 hours.
**Servings:** 4
**Ingredients:**

- 2 cups brown rice, soaked in water overnight, drained, and rinsed

- ½ small onion, chopped
- 4 cups vegetable broth
- 2 tablespoons extra-virgin olive oil
- ½ teaspoon dried thyme leaves
- ½ teaspoon garlic powder
- ½ cup cooked sliced mushrooms
- ½ cup dried cranberries
- ½ cup toasted pecans

**Directions:**
1. In your slow cooker, combine the rice, onion, broth, olive oil, thyme, and garlic powder. Stir well.
2. Cover the cooker then set to high. Cook for almost 3 hours.
3. Stir in the mushrooms, cranberries, and pecans, and serve.

**Per serving:** Calories: 313kcal; Fat: 8.2g; Carbs: 50.8g; Protein: 8.4g

## 46. Vegetable Broth

**Preparation time:** 15 minutes.
**Cooking time:** 8 hours.
**Servings:** 12
**Ingredients:**

- Olive oil, for coating the slow cooker
- 6 cups veggie scraps (peels and pieces of carrots, celery, onions, garlic)
- 12 cups filtered water
- ½ medium onion, chopped
- 2 garlic cloves, chopped
- 1 parsley sprig
- ¾ teaspoon sea salt
- ½ teaspoon dried oregano
- ½ teaspoon dried basil leaves
- 2 bay leaves

**Directions:**
1. Layer the slow cooker with a thin layer of olive oil.
2. In the slow cooker, combine the veggie scraps, water, onion, garlic, parsley, salt, oregano, basil, and bay leaves.
3. Cover the cooker then set to low. Cook for almost 6 to 8 hours.
4. Pour the broth through a fine-mesh sieve. Set over a suitable bowl, discarding the veggie scraps. Refrigerate the broth in airtight containers for up to 5 days, or freeze for up to 3 months.

**Per serving:** Calories: 104kcal; Fat: 0.4g; Carbs: 23.1g; Protein: 4.4g

## 47. Grain-Free Salad Bowl

**Preparation time:** 10 minutes.
**Cooking time:** 5 minutes.
**Servings:** 4
**Ingredients:**

- ½ cup chopped walnuts
- ¼ cup chopped pistachios
- ¼ cup raw pumpkin seeds or sunflower seeds
- 4 cups baby arugula or spinach leaves
- 2 cups riced cauliflower (not frozen)
- 1 large seedless cucumber, peeled and chopped
- 4 roma tomatoes, seeded and chopped
- ½ cup chopped parsley or cilantro
- ¼ cup chopped red onion
- ¼ cup extra-virgin olive oil
- 2 tablespoons apple cider vinegar
- 1 teaspoon salt
- ¼ teaspoon black pepper, freshly ground

**Directions:**
1. In a huge dry skillet, toast the walnuts, pistachios, and pumpkin seeds over medium-low heat for almost 5 minutes, until the nuts and seeds are

golden and fragrant. Remove from this skillet and set aside to cool.
2. In a suitable bowl, combine the arugula, cauliflower, cucumber, tomatoes, parsley, and onion.
3. In a suitable bowl, whisk together the olive oil, vinegar, salt, and pepper. Add the cooled nuts and seeds to the vegetable bowl, drizzle with the oil mixture, and toss to coat well.
4. Divide among bowls and serve chilled or at room temperature.

**Per serving:** Calories: 364kcal; Fat: 33.4g; Carbs: 14.5g; Protein: 7.8g

## 48. Stuffed Sweet Potatoes

**Preparation time:** 15 minutes.
**Cooking time:** 7 hours.
**Servings:** 4
**Ingredients:**

- 4 medium sweet potatoes
- 1 cup hatch chile "refried" beans
- 4 tablespoons chopped scallions (both white and green parts)
- 1 avocado, peeled, pitted, and quartered

**Directions:**
1. Wash the sweet potatoes, but do not dry them. The water left on the skins from washing is the only moisture needed for cooking. Put the damp sweet potatoes in your slow cooker.
2. Cover the cooker then set to low. Cook for almost 6 to 7 hours. A fork should easily poke through when they are done.
3. Carefully remove the hot sweet potatoes from the slow cooker. Slice each one lengthwise about halfway through. Mash the revealed flesh with a fork, and fill the opening with ¼ cup of beans. Top each with 1 tablespoon of scallions and a quarter of the avocado and serve.

**Per serving:** Calories: 281kcal; Fat: 10.1g; Carbs: 46.6g; Protein: 3.4g

## 49. Split Pea Carrot Soup

**Preparation time:** 15 minutes.
**Cooking time:** 8 hours.
**Servings:** 4 to 6
**Ingredients:**

- 2 cups dried split peas, soaked in water overnight, drained, and rinsed well
- 3 carrots, chopped
- 1 celery stalk, diced
- ½ medium onion, diced
- 1 tablespoon extra-virgin olive oil
- 1 tablespoon lemon juice, freshly squeezed
- 2 teaspoons dried thyme leaves
- 1 teaspoon garlic powder
- ½ teaspoon dried oregano
- 2 bay leaves
- 8 cups broth (choose vegetable to keep it vegan)

**Directions:**
1. In your slow cooker, combine the split peas, carrots, celery, onion, olive oil, lemon juice, thyme, garlic powder, oregano, bay leaves, and broth.
2. Cover the cooker then set to low. Cook for 7 to 8 hours.
3. Remove and discard the bay leaves. For a smoother soup, blend with an immersion blender and serve.

**Per serving:** Calories: 315kcal; Fat: 5g; Carbs: 45.5g; Protein: 23.1g

## 50. Spanish Rice

**Preparation time:** 15 minutes.
**Cooking time:** 6 hours.
**Servings:** 4 to 6

**Ingredients:**
- 2 cups white rice
- 2 cups vegetable broth
- 2 tablespoons extra-virgin olive oil
- 1 (15-ounce) can crushed tomatoes
- 1 (4-ounce) can hatch green chiles
- ½ medium onion, diced
- 1 teaspoon sea salt
- ½ teaspoon ground cumin
- ½ teaspoon garlic powder
- ½ teaspoon chili powder
- ½ teaspoon dried oregano
- Black pepper

**Directions:**
1. In your slow cooker, combine the rice, broth, olive oil, tomatoes, chiles, onion, salt, cumin, garlic powder, chili powder, and oregano, and season with pepper.
2. Cover the cooker then set to low. Cook for almost 5 to 6 hours, fluff, and serve.

**Per serving:** Calories: 313kcal; Fat: 5.6g; Carbs: 56.6g; Protein: 7.9g

## 51. Fried Quinoa

**Preparation time:** 15 minutes.
**Cooking time:** 6 hours.
**Servings:** 4 to 6
**Ingredients:**
- 2 cups quinoa, rinsed well
- 4 cups vegetable broth
- ¼ cup sliced carrots
- ¼ cup corn kernels
- ¼ cup green peas
- ¼ cup diced scallion
- 1 tablespoon sesame oil
- 1 teaspoon garlic powder
- 1 teaspoon sea salt
- Dash red pepper flakes

**Directions:**
1. In your slow cooker, combine the quinoa, broth, carrots, corn, peas, scallion, sesame oil, garlic powder, salt, and red pepper flakes.
2. Cover the cooker then set to low. Cook for almost 4 to 6 hours, fluff, and serve.

**Per serving:** Calories: 270kcal; Fat: 6.7g; Carbs: 40.2g; Protein: 12g

## 52. Mushroom Risotto

**Preparation time:** 15 minutes.
**Cooking time:** 3 hours.
**Servings:** 4
**Ingredients:**
- 1½ cups arborio rice
- 1 cup English peas
- 1 small shallot, minced
- ¼ cup dried porcini mushrooms
- 4½ cups broth (choose vegetable to keep it vegan)
- 1 tablespoon lemon juice
- ½ teaspoon garlic powder
- ½ teaspoon sea salt

**Directions:**
1. In your slow cooker, combine the rice, peas, shallot, mushrooms, broth, lemon juice, garlic powder, and salt. Stir to mix well.
2. Cover the cooker then set to high. Cook for almost 2 to 3 hours and serve.

**Per serving:** Calories: 223kcal; Fat: 1.4g; Carbs: 42.5g; Protein: 8.2g

# CHAPTER 3: Fish and Seafoods

## 53. Basic Shrimp

**Preparation time:** 15 minutes.

**Cooking time:** 0 minutes.
**Servings:** 4
**Ingredients:**

- 12 frozen jumbo shrimp, in shells

**Directions:**

1. Pour 1½ cups water into your Instant pot and set the steam rack inside. Add the shrimp to your steamer basket and place it on the rack. Close the lid and secure it well.
2. Hit the the manual cook button and adjust the time to 0 minutes.
3. When cooked, release the pressure quickly until the float valve drops and then unlock lid.

**Per serving:** Calories: 120kcal; Fat: 2g; Carbs: 1g; Protein: 23g

### 54. Mediterranean Fish Stew

**Preparation time:** 15 minutes
**Cooking time:** 15 minutes
**Servings:** 4
**Ingredients:**

- 1 tablespoon olive oil
- 1 white onion, sliced thin
- 1 fennel bulb, sliced thin
- 2 garlic cloves, minced
- 1 (28-ounce) can crushed tomatoes
- Pinch saffron threads
- 1 teaspoon ground cumin
- 1 teaspoon ground oregano
- 1 teaspoon salt
- ½ teaspoon black pepper
- 2 pounds firm white fish fillets, cut into 2-inch pieces
- 2 tablespoons fresh parsley, chopped
- ½ lemon, for garnish

**Directions:**

1. In a suitable pot or pan, heat 1 tablespoon of olive oil over medium-high heat. Add the onion, fennel, and garlic, sauté them for 5 minutes.
2. Stir in the crushed tomatoes, saffron threads, cumin, oregano, salt, and pepper. Bring the mixture to a simmer.
3. Lay the prepared fish fillets in a single layer over the vegetables, cover the pan, and simmer for 10 minutes.
4. Transfer the fish and vegetables to your serving platter. Garnish with the parsley, a drizzle of olive oil, and a generous squeeze of lemon juice.

**Per serving:** Calories: 535kcal; Fat: 21g; Carbs: 24g; Protein: 62g

### 55. Tuna Salad With Brown Rice

**Preparation time:** 15 minutes.
**Cooking time:** 15 minutes.
**Servings:** 4
**Ingredients:**

- 1 cup brown rice
- 1 cup water
- Pinch sea salt
- 1 ripe avocado, peeled, halved, and pitted
- 2 (3-ounce) cans water-packed tuna, drained and rinsed
- 1 red bell pepper, diced
- 1 cucumber, seeded and diced
- 1 scallion, white and green parts, sliced, then minced
- 2 tablespoons capers, drained
- Juice of 1 small lemon

**Directions:**

1. In the instant pot, combine the brown rice, water, and salt. Lock the lid.
2. Pressure cook at high for almost 15 minutes.
3. In a suitable bowl, using a fork, mash the avocado until creamy. Add the tuna to the bowl, then add the bell

pepper, cucumber, scallion, and capers. Mix until combined well.
4. When cooked, use a natural release for almost 5 minutes, then quick release any remaining pressure. Turn off the heat.
5. Remove the lid and pour the tuna mixture into the pot and stir to combine with the rice.
6. Stir in the lemon juice then serve immediately, or refrigerate in an airtight container for up to 4 days.

**Per serving:** Calories: 347kcal; Fat: 11.6g; Carbs: 46g; Protein: 16.3g

## 56. Lemon Dill Salmon

**Preparation time:** 15 minutes.
**Cooking time:** 3 minutes.
**Servings:** 4
**Ingredients:**

- 4 (4", 6-ounce) salmon filets
- 1 teaspoon avocado oil
- Juice of 1 medium lemon
- 1 teaspoon dried dill weed
- ½ teaspoon salt

**Directions:**
1. Brush the salmon filets with oil, then top with the lemon juice, dill weed, and salt.
2. Add 1 cup water to your instant pot and set the steam rack inside. Set the salmon filets on top of the steam rack. Close the lid and secure it well.
3. Hit the the manual cook button and adjust the time to 3 minutes.
4. When cooked, release the pressure quickly until the float valve drops and then unlock lid. Serve immediately.

**Per serving:** Calories: 282kcal; Fat: 12.7g; Carbs: 0.2g; Protein: 39.2g

## 57. Power Poke Bowl

**Preparation time:** 15 minutes.
**Cooking time:** 0 minutes.
**Servings:** 4
**Ingredients:**

- ¼ cup tamari
- ¼ cup sesame oil
- 1 tablespoon minced fresh ginger, or ½ teaspoon ground ginger
- 1 to 2 teaspoons red pepper flakes
- 8 ounces sashimi-grade tuna or smoked salmon, cut into bite-size cubes
- ¼ cup anti-inflammatory mayo
- 2 tablespoons rice vinegar or lime juice
- 1 to 2 teaspoons sriracha or other hot sauce
- 4 cups mixed greens
- ¼ cup chopped fresh cilantro or basil
- 1 avocado, sliced
- 8 thin slices cucumber
- ¼ cup sliced scallions, white and green parts
- 2 teaspoons sesame seeds

**Directions:**
1. In a suitable bowl, whisk together the tamari, sesame oil, ginger, and red pepper flakes. Add the tuna, toss to coat, cover and refrigerate for at least 30 minutes or up to overnight.
2. While the tuna marinates, in a suitable bowl whisk together the mayo, vinegar, and sriracha. Set aside.
3. To prepare the bowls, divide the salad greens and cilantro between bowls. Top with the avocado, cucumber, and scallions. Add half of the marinated tuna mixture and the liquid to each bowl.
4. Drizzle with the spicy mayonnaise mixture and sesame seeds. Serve immediately.

**Per serving:** Calories: 352kcal; Fat: 18.4g; Carbs: 35g; Protein: 15.2g

**Per serving:** Calories: 312kcal; Fat: 25g; Carbs: 3.1g; Protein: 19.3g

## 58. Seared Citrus Scallops With Mint And Basil

**Preparation time:** 15 minutes.
**Cooking time:** 10 minutes.
**Servings:** 4
**Ingredients:**

- 1 pound sea scallops, patted dry
- 1 teaspoon salt
- ½ teaspoon black pepper
- ¼ cup extra-virgin olive oil
- 4 tablespoons grass-fed butter
- Grated zest and juice of 1 orange
- Grated zest and juice of 1 lemon
- 2 tablespoons chopped fresh mint
- 2 tablespoons chopped fresh basil

**Directions:**

1. Sprinkle the scallops with ½ teaspoon of salt and the pepper.
2. In a suitable skillet, heat the olive oil over medium-high heat. Set the scallops, one by one, into the hot oil and sear for almost 2 to 3 minutes on each side until the scallops are lightly golden. Using a slotted spoon, remove from this skillet and keep warm.
3. Add the butter to this skillet and reduce its heat to medium low. Once the butter has melted, whisk in the citrus zests and juices, mint, basil, and the rest of the ½ teaspoon of salt. Cook for almost 1 minute.
4. Remove from the heat then return the seared scallops to this skillet, tossing to layer them in the butter sauce.
5. Serve the scallops warm, drizzled with sauce.

## 59. Seared Cod With Mushroom Sauce

**Preparation time:** 15 minutes.
**Cooking time:** 20 minutes.
**Servings:** 4
**Ingredients:**

- 1 pound cod fillet
- ½ teaspoon salt
- ¼ teaspoon black pepper
- ½ cup coconut oil
- Grated zest and juice of 1 lime
- 4 ounces shiitake mushrooms, sliced
- 2 garlic cloves, minced
- 1 (15-ounce) can full-fat coconut milk
- 1 teaspoon ground ginger
- 1 teaspoon red pepper flakes
- 2 tablespoons tamari (or 1 tablespoon miso paste and 1 tablespoon water)
- 2 tablespoons toasted sesame oil

**Directions:**

1. Cut the cod into four equal pieces and season with black pepper and salt.
2. In a suitable skillet, heat 4 tablespoons of coconut oil over high heat until just before smoking.
3. Add the cod, skin-side up, cover to prevent splattering and sear for almost 4 to 5 minutes, until it's golden brown. Remove the fish from this skillet, drizzle with the juice of ½ lime, and let rest.
4. In the same skillet, add the rest of the 4 tablespoons of coconut oil and heat over medium. Add the mushrooms and sauté for almost 5 to 6 minutes, until they are just tender. Add the

garlic and sauté for almost 1 minute, until fragrant.
5. Whisk in the coconut milk, ginger, red pepper flakes, tamari, and remaining lime zest and juice.
6. Reduce its heat to low. Return the cod to this skillet, skin-side down, cover and simmer for almost 3 to 4 minutes, until the fish is cooked through.
7. To serve, set the cod on rimmed plates or in shallow bowls and spoon the sauce over the fish. Drizzle with the sesame oil.

**Per serving:** Calories: 470kcal; Fat: 41.2g; Carbs: 6.1g; Protein: 22.2g

## 60. Seafood Stew

**Preparation time:** 15 minutes.
**Cooking time:** 18 minutes.
**Servings:** 4
**Ingredients:**
- 1½ pounds Yukon gold potatoes, diced
- 1 (15-ounce) can diced tomatoes
- 2 red bell peppers, chopped
- 1 yellow onion, chopped
- 4 garlic cloves, minced
- 2 teaspoons sea salt
- 1 cup water
- ½ cup apple cider vinegar
- 2 cups chopped cod or halibut
- 10 raw shrimp, peeled and deveined
- 1 cup bay scallops
- 6 ounces clam meat, rinsed

**Directions:**
1. In the instant pot, combine the potatoes, tomatoes with their juices, bell peppers, onion, garlic, salt, water, and vinegar. Lock the lid.
2. Select pressure cook and cook at high pressure for almost 15 minutes.
3. When cooking is complete, use a natural release for almost 10 minutes, then quick release any remaining pressure. Turn off the heat. Remove the lid.
4. Select sauté on your instant pot and add the cod, shrimp, scallops, and clam meat. Cook for almost 3 minutes, while stirring frequently. Remove and serve.

**Per serving:** Calories: 402kcal; Fat: 5.7g; Carbs: 21.8g; Protein: 62.3g

## 61. Herbed Salmon Orzo Antipasto

**Preparation time:** 15 minutes.
**Cooking time:** 7 minutes.
**Servings:** 4
**Ingredients:**
- 2 tablespoons avocado oil
- 1½ cups orzo
- 1 small yellow onion, diced
- 3 garlic cloves, minced
- 2¾ cups vegetable broth
- 1 cup diced tomatoes
- ¼ cup fresh basil, chopped
- 2 teaspoons sea salt
- 1 teaspoon Italian seasoning
- 1 cup water
- 1 pound salmon fillets
- ½ teaspoon black pepper
- 1 tablespoon extra-virgin olive oil
- 2 tablespoons chopped fresh parsley

**Directions:**
1. Select sauté on your instant pot and let the pot preheat.
2. Add the avocado oil, orzo, onion, and garlic. Cook for almost 3 minutes.
3. Stir in the broth, tomatoes, basil, 1 teaspoon of salt, and the Italian seasoning to combine. Turn off the heat. Lock the lid.

4. Pressure cook at high for almost 3 minutes.
5. When cooked, use a quick release.
6. Remove the lid and transfer the cooked orzo to a suitable bowl, cover, and set aside.
7. Place a metal trivet or steam rack in the instant pot and pour in the water. Set the salmon fillets on the trivet in a single layer and season with the rest of the 1 teaspoon of salt and the pepper. Lock the lid.
8. Pressure cook at high for almost 1 minute.
9. When cooked, use a quick release.
10. Remove the lid and, using a spatula, transfer the cooked salmon to a cutting board. Using two forks, shred the salmon and let cool. Once cooled, add the salmon to the orzo and stir well to combine.
11. Drizzle with the olive oil and top with the parsley to serve.

**Per serving:** Calories: 46kcal; Fat: 13.6g; Carbs: 53g; Protein: 32.9g

## 62. Rainbow Trout

**Preparation time:** 15 minutes.
**Cooking time:** 2 minutes.
**Servings:** 4
**Ingredients:**

- 2 carrots, chopped
- 2 celery stalks, chopped
- 1 cup broccoli florets, diced
- 1 cup cauliflower florets, diced
- 1 pound rainbow trout fillets
- ¼ cup water
- 1 teaspoon sea salt
- ¼ teaspoon paprika
- ¼ teaspoon black pepper
- 2 tablespoons ghee
- 1 lemon, cut into wedges
- 1 tablespoon chopped fresh parsley

**Directions:**
1. In the instant pot, combine the carrots, celery, broccoli, and cauliflower. Put a metal trivet or steam rack on top of the vegetables so it lies flat. Set the trout on the trivet and pour the water over the fish. Sprinkle the fish with the salt, paprika, and pepper. Set the ghee and lemon wedges on top of the fish. Lock the lid.
2. Select pressure cook and cook at high pressure for almost 2 minutes.
3. When cooking is complete, use a quick release.
4. Remove the lid. Using potholders, remove the trivet and transfer the steamed trout to a serving dish. Spoon the vegetables onto the dish and sprinkle with the parsley to serve.

**Per serving:** Calories: 219kcal; Fat: 14.6g; Carbs: 10.7g; Protein: 14.7g

## 63. Buckwheat Ramen With Cod

**Preparation time:** 15 minutes.
**Cooking time:** 2 minutes.
**Servings:** 4
**Ingredients:**
For the ramen

- 6 ounces buckwheat ramen
- 5 ounces shiitake or cremini mushrooms, sliced
- 4 garlic cloves, minced
- 1 yellow onion, diced
- 4 cups low-sodium vegetable broth
- ¼ cup tamari
- 2 tablespoons apple cider vinegar
- 3 cups chopped cod fillet

For serving

- 4 soft-boiled eggs

- 2 teaspoons toasted sesame seeds

**Directions:**
1. To make the ramen: in the instant pot, combine the noodles, mushrooms, garlic, onion, broth, tamari, and vinegar. Lock the lid.
2. Select pressure cook and cook at high pressure for almost 2 minutes.
3. When cooked, use a natural release for almost 4 minutes, then quick release any remaining pressure.
4. Remove the lid and add the cod. Cook, while stirring, for almost 2 minutes in keep warm mode until the fish is cooked to your desired doneness.
5. To serve: divide the noodles, fish, and broth into serving bowls. Top each with a soft-boiled egg and a sprinkle of the sesame seeds.

**Per serving:** Calories: 481kcal; Fat: 4.1g; Carbs: 70.5g; Protein: 40.5g

## 64. Shrimp Balls Over Garlicky Greens

**Preparation time:** 15 minutes.
**Cooking time:** 25 minutes.
**Servings:** 4
**Ingredients:**

- 1 pound wild-caught shrimp, peeled, deveined, and chopped
- ¼ cup coconut or almond flour
- 1 large egg, lightly beaten
- 1 (2-inch) piece fresh ginger, peeled and minced
- ¼ cup minced scallion, green part only
- 1 teaspoon garlic powder
- Grated zest of 1 lime
- ½ teaspoon salt
- ¼ to ½ teaspoon red pepper flakes
- 10 tablespoons extra-virgin olive oil, more for frying as needed
- 8 cups kale or spinach, torn into bite-size pieces
- 6 garlic cloves, minced
- ¼ cup soy sauce
- 2 tablespoons rice vinegar
- 2 tablespoons sesame oil

**Directions:**
1. In a suitable bowl, combine the shrimp, coconut flour, egg, ginger, 2 tablespoons of scallion, garlic powder, lime zest, salt, and red pepper flakes, mixing well with a fork. Using your hands, form the shrimp mixture into about a dozen (1-inch) balls and place them on your cutting board or baking sheet lined with parchment paper. Allow to rest for almost 10 minutes.
2. In a mini skillet or saucepan, heat 4 tablespoons of olive oil over medium-high heat. Working in batches of three to four balls, panfry them for almost 5 to 7 minutes total, carefully turning to brown all sides. Repeat until all the shrimp balls have been fried, adding additional oil with each batch as needed. Keep the shrimp balls warm.
3. In a suitable skillet, heat 2 tablespoons of olive oil over medium-high heat. Add the greens and sauté for almost 5 minutes. Add the garlic and sauté for almost 2 to 4 minutes until the greens are wilted.
4. In a suitable bowl, whisk together the soy sauce, vinegar, and sesame oil.
5. To serve, divide the sautéed greens between plates and top with three shrimp balls drizzled with the sauce.

**Per serving:** Calories: 413kcal; Fat: 33.5g; Carbs: 20g; Protein: 4.9g

## 65. Shrimp Paella

**Preparation time:** 15 minutes.
**Cooking time:** 14 minutes.

**Servings:** 4
**Ingredients:**
- 2 tablespoons avocado oil
- 1 medium white onion, peeled and chopped
- 4 garlic cloves, chopped
- 1 teaspoon paprika
- 1 teaspoon turmeric
- ½ teaspoon salt
- ¼ teaspoon black pepper
- Pinch saffron threads
- ¼ teaspoon red pepper flakes
- 1 cup jasmine rice
- 1 cup chicken stock
- 1 pound frozen jumbo shrimp, shell and tail on
- ¼ cup chopped fresh cilantro

**Directions:**
1. Press the sauté button and add the oil to the inner pot. Allow it to heat 2 minutes, and then add the onion and cook until softened, about 5 minutes.
2. Add the garlic, paprika, turmeric, salt, black pepper, saffron, and red pepper flakes and sauté another 30 seconds. Add the rice, stir, and cook 1 more minute.
3. Add the stock and stir, and use a spoon to make sure there are no brown bits stuck to the bottom of your pot. Add the shrimp. Close the lid and secure it well.
4. Hit the the manual cook button and adjust the time to 5 minutes.
5. When cooked, release the pressure quickly until the float valve drops and then unlock lid.
6. Remove the prepared mixture from the pot and peel the shrimp if desired.
7. Serve garnished with cilantro.

**Per serving:** Calories: 312kcal; Fat: 3.2g; Carbs: 42g; Protein: 26.9g

## 66. Garlic Shrimp And Broccoli

**Preparation time:** 15 minutes.
**Cooking time:** 5 minutes.
**Servings:** 4
**Ingredients:**
- 2 tablespoons avocado oil
- 2 medium shallots, peeled and diced
- 1 tablespoon minced garlic
- ¾ cup chicken stock
- 1½ tablespoons lemon juice
- ½ teaspoon kosher salt
- ½ teaspoon black pepper
- 1½ pounds peeled, deveined jumbo shrimp
- 2½ cups small broccoli florets

**Directions:**
1. Press the sauté button and add the oil to the inner pot. Allow it to heat 1 minute and then add the shallots. Cook the shallots 3 minutes and then add the garlic and continue to cook an additional 1 minute.
2. Add the stock and use a spoon to remove any brown bits that are stuck to the pot.
3. Add the lemon juice, salt, pepper, and shrimp. Then add the broccoli to the top layer and do not stir. Close the lid and secure it well.
4. Hit the the manual cook button and adjust the time to 0 minutes.
5. When cooked, release the pressure quickly until the float valve drops and then unlock lid.

**Per serving:** Calories: 335kcal; Fat: 2.2g; Carbs: 84.6g; Protein: 3.7g

# CHAPTER 4: Chicken and Poultry

## 67. Chicken Tenders With Mustard Sauce

**Preparation time:** 5 minutes.
**Cooking time:** 7 minutes.
**Servings:** 4
**Ingredients:**

- 1 pound chicken tenders
- 1 tablespoon fresh thyme leaves
- ½ teaspoon salt
- ¼ teaspoon black pepper
- 1 tablespoon avocado oil
- 1 cup chicken stock
- ¼ cup Dijon mustard
- ¼ cup raw honey

**Directions:**

1. Dry the chicken tenders with a towel and then season them with the thyme, salt, and pepper.
2. Press the sauté button and then use the adjust button to change to the more setting. Add the oil to your Instant pot and let it heat 2 minutes. Add the chicken tenders and seer them until brown on both sides, about 1 minute per side. Turn off heat.
3. Remove the chicken tenders and set aside. Add the stock to the pot. Use a spoon to scrape up any small bits from the bottom of the pot.
4. Set the steam rack in your Instant pot and set the chicken tenders directly on the rack. Close the lid and secure it well.
5. Pressure cook for 3 minutes.
6. In a suitable bowl, combine the Dijon mustard and honey and stir to combine.
7. Once done, release the presssure naturally then remove the lid. Serve the chicken tenders with the honey mustard sauce.

**Per serving:** Calories: 300kcal; Fat: 9.7g; Carbs: 19.2g; Protein: 33.8g

## 68. Chicken Breasts With Mushrooms

**Preparation time:** 10 minutes.
**Cooking time:** 18 minutes.
**Servings:** 4
**Ingredients:**

- 2 tablespoons avocado oil
- 1 pound sliced baby bella mushrooms
- 1½ teaspoons salt
- 2 garlic cloves, minced
- 8 cups chopped green cabbage
- 1½ teaspoons dried thyme
- ½ cup chicken stock
- 1½ pounds chicken breasts, boneless, skinless

**Directions:**

1. Heat the oil to your Instant pot and allow it to heat 1 minute. Add the mushrooms and ¼ teaspoon salt and sauté until they have cooked down and released their liquid, about 10 minutes.
2. Add the garlic and sauté another 30 seconds. Turn off heat.
3. Add the cabbage, ¼ teaspoon salt, thyme, and stock to your Instant pot and stir to combine.
4. Dry the chicken breasts and sprinkle both sides with the rest of the salt. Place on top of the cabbage mixture. Close the lid and secure it well.

5. Pressure cook for 6 minutes approximately.
6. Once cooked, release the presssure naturally then remove the lid.
7. Transfer to plates and spoon the juices on top.

**Per serving:** Calories: 404kcal; Fat: 14g; Carbs: 15.7g; Protein: 54.3g

## 69. Rosemary Chicken

**Preparation time:** 15 minutes.
**Cooking time:** 20 minutes.
**Servings:** 4
**Ingredients:**

- 1½ pounds chicken breast tenders
- 2 tablespoons extra-virgin olive oil
- 2 tablespoons chopped fresh rosemary leaves
- ½ teaspoon sea salt
- ⅛ teaspoon black pepper

**Directions:**
1. At 425 degrees F, preheat your oven.
2. Set the chicken tenders on a rimmed baking sheet. Brush them with the olive oil and sprinkle with the rosemary, salt, and pepper.
3. Bake for almost 15 to 20 minutes until the juices run clear.

**Per serving:** Calories: 415kcal; Fat: 6.7g; Carbs: 0.7g; Protein: 81.7g

## 70. Jerk Chicken

**Preparation time:** 15 minutes.
**Cooking time:** 22 minutes.
**Servings:** 8
**Ingredients:**

- 1 large onion, peeled
- 1 tablespoon peeled and chopped fresh ginger
- 3 small hot chili peppers, deveined and deseeded
- ½ teaspoon ground allspice
- 2 tablespoons dry mustard
- 1 teaspoon black pepper
- 2 tablespoons red wine vinegar
- 2 tablespoons coconut aminos
- 2 garlic cloves, minced
- ½ cup chicken stock
- 4 pounds skinless chicken breasts, boneless, cut in 1" pieces

**Directions:**
1. Cut the onion into 8 pieces.
2. Combine all the recipe ingredients except the chicken in a food processor or blender and process until liquefied.
3. Add the chicken to your instant pot, top with the sauce, and stir to combine. Close the lid and secure it well.
4. Pressure cook for 12 minutes.
5. When cooked, release the pressure quickly until the float valve drops and then unlock lid.
6. Remove the chicken from instant pot and spread on a baking sheet lined with parchment paper or a silicone baking mat. Drizzle sauce over the chicken.
7. Serve as is, or for a golden-browned finish, set broiler to high and broil 6–10 minutes, turning once 'til chicken is nicely browned.

**Per serving:** Calories: 455kcal; Fat: 17.7g; Carbs: 3.3g; Protein: 66.7g

## 71. Spiced Chicken Vegetables

**Preparation time:** 15 minutes.
**Cooking time:** 15 minutes.
**Servings:** 4
**Ingredients:**

- 1 teaspoon dried thyme
- ¼ teaspoon ground ginger

- ¼ teaspoon ground allspice
- 1 teaspoon kosher salt
- ½ teaspoon black pepper
- 2 large bone-in chicken breasts (about 2 pounds)
- ½ cup chicken stock
- 2 medium onions, peeled and cut in fourths
- 4 medium carrots

**Directions:**
1. In a suitable bowl, mix together the thyme, ginger, allspice, salt, and pepper.
2. Use half of the spice mixture to season the chicken breasts.
3. Pour the chicken stock into your Instant pot and then add the chicken breasts. Set the onions and carrots on top of the chicken and sprinkle them with the rest of the seasoning blend. Close the lid and secure it well.
4. Pressure cook for 15 minutes.
5. Once cooked, release the presssure naturally then remove the lid.
6. Remove the chicken and the vegetables and serve alone or with rice or lentils.

**Per serving:** Calories: 156kcal; Fat: 2.3g; Carbs: 11.7g; Protein: 21.6g

### 72. Chicken Adobo

**Preparation time:** 5 minutes.
**Cooking time:** 15 minutes.
**Servings:** 4
**Ingredients:**

- 3 tablespoons extra-viegin olive oil
- 1½ pounds skinless, boneless chicken breasts, diced
- 2 teaspoons ground turmeric
- ¼ cup low-sodium soy sauce
- 1 teaspoon garlic powder
- 1 teaspoon onion powder
- ½ teaspoon sea salt
- ¼ teaspoon black pepper

**Directions:**
1. In a suitable skillet over medium-high heat, heat the olive oil until it shimmers.
2. Add the chicken and turmeric. Cook for almost 7 to 10 minutes, while stirring occasionally, until the chicken is cooked through.
3. Stir in the soy sauce, garlic powder, onion powder, salt, and pepper. Cook for almost 3 minutes, while stirring.

**Per serving:** Calories: 427kcal; Fat: 23.2g; Carbs: 2.8g; Protein: 50.5g

### 73. Chicken Cacciatore

**Preparation time:** 5 minutes.
**Cooking time:** 20 minutes.
**Servings:** 4
**Ingredients:**

- 2 tablespoons olive oil
- 1½ pounds skinless, boneless chicken breasts, diced
- 2 (28-ounce) cans crushed tomatoes, drained
- ½ cup black olives, chopped
- 1 teaspoon garlic powder
- 1 teaspoon onion powder
- ½ teaspoon sea salt
- ⅛ teaspoon black pepper, freshly ground

**Directions:**
1. In a suitable skillet over medium-high heat, heat the olive oil until it shimmers.
2. Add the chicken and cook for 7 to 10 minutes, while stirring occasionally, until it is browned.

3. Stir in the tomatoes, olives, garlic powder, onion powder, salt, and pepper. Simmer for almost 10 minutes, while stirring occasionally.

**Per serving:** Calories: 432kcal; Fat: 21.4g; Carbs: 7g; Protein: 51g

## 74. Turkey Meatloaf

**Preparation time:** 15 minutes.
**Cooking time:** 25 minutes.
**Servings:** 4
**Ingredients:**
- 1 tablespoon avocado oil
- 1 small onion, peeled and diced
- 2 garlic cloves, minced
- 3 cups mixed baby greens, chopped
- 1 pound lean ground turkey
- ¼ cup almond flour
- 1 large egg
- ¾ teaspoon salt
- ½ teaspoon black pepper

**Directions:**
1. Add the oil to your inner pot. Heat the oil 1 minute.
2. Add the onion and sauté until softened, 3 minutes. Add the garlic and greens and sauté 1 more minute. Turn off heat.
3. In a suitable bowl, combine the turkey, flour, egg, salt, and pepper.
4. Add the onion and greens mixture to the turkey mixture and stir to combine.
5. Rinse out your Instant pot and then add 2 cups water.
6. Make an aluminum foil sling by folding a large piece of foil in half and bending the edges upward.
7. Form the turkey mixture into a rectangular loaf and place it on the aluminum foil sling. Set the sling onto the steam rack with handles, and lower it into the inner pot. Close the lid and secure it well.
8. Pressure cook for 20 minutes.
9. When cooked, release the pressure quickly until the float valve drops and then unlock lid.
10. Carefully remove the meatloaf from your Instant pot and allow it to rest for almost 10 minutes before slicing to serve.

**Per serving:** Calories: 263kcal; Fat: 13.2g; Carbs: 9.4g; Protein: 28g

## 75. Avocado Chicken Salad

**Preparation time:** 10 minutes.
**Cooking time:** 6 minutes approximately.
**Servings:** 4
**Ingredients:**
- 1 pound skinless chicken breasts, boneless
- ½ cup chicken stock
- 1½ medium avocados, peeled, pitted, and mashed
- 1 medium stalk celery, ends removed and diced
- 1 scallion, sliced
- 1 tablespoon lemon juice
- 1 tablespoon chopped fresh parsley
- ½ teaspoon dried dill weed
- 2 teaspoons Dijon mustard
- ½ teaspoon kosher salt
- ¼ teaspoon black pepper

**Directions:**
1. Add the chicken breasts and stock to your Instant Pot. Close the lid and secure it.
2. Pressure cook for 6 minutes approximately.

3. Once cooked, release the presssure naturally then remove the lid.
4. Remove the chicken from your instant pot and let it cool down completely. Once it is cool, chop the chicken.
5. Set the chopped chicken in a suitable bowl and add the rest of the ingredients. Stir to combine.

**Per serving:** Calories: 336kcal; Fat: 19.6g; Carbs: 5.6g; Protein: 34.3g

## 76. Tuscan Chicken

**Preparation time:** 5 minutes.
**Cooking time:** 20 minutes.
**Servings:** 4
**Ingredients:**

- 4 skinless, boneless chicken breast halves, pounded to ½- to ¾-inch thickness
- ½ teaspoon sea salt
- ⅛ teaspoon black pepper
- 1 teaspoon garlic powder
- 2 tablespoons extra-virgin olive oil
- 1 zucchini, chopped
- 2 cups cherry tomatoes
- ½ cup sliced green olives
- ¼ cup dry white wine

**Directions:**
1. Rub the chicken breasts with the salt, pepper, and garlic powder.
2. In a suitable skillet over medium-high heat, heat the olive oil until it shimmers. Stir in the chicken and cook 7 to 10 minutes per side, until it reaches an internal temperature of 165°F.
3. Remove the cooked chicken then set aside on a platter, tented with foil.
4. In the same skillet, add the zucchini, tomatoes, and olives. Cook for almost 4 minutes, while stirring occasionally, until the zucchini is tender.
5. Add the white wine and use a spoon to scrape any browned bits from the bottom of this pan. Simmer for almost 1 minute. Return the cooked chicken and any juices that have collected on the platter to this pan and stir to coat with the sauce and vegetables.

**Per serving:** Calories: 366kcal; Fat: 17.8g; Carbs: 6.2g; Protein: 42g

## 77. Turkey With Bell Peppers And Rosemary

**Preparation time:** 15 minutes.
**Cooking time:** 10 minutes.
**Servings:** 4
**Ingredients:**

- 3 tablespoons extra-virgin olive oil
- 2 red bell peppers, chopped
- 1 onion, chopped
- 1½ pounds skinless, boneless turkey breasts, diced
- 2 tablespoons chopped fresh rosemary leaves
- ½ teaspoon sea salt
- ⅛ teaspoon black pepper
- 3 garlic cloves, minced

**Directions:**
1. In a suitable skillet over medium-high heat, heat the olive oil until it shimmers.
2. Add the red bell peppers, onion, turkey, rosemary, salt, and pepper. Cook for 7 to 10 minutes, while stirring occasionally, until the turkey is cooked and the vegetables are tender.
3. Add the garlic. Cook for almost 30 seconds more, while stirring constantly.

**Per serving:** Calories: 389kcal; Fat: 10.7g; Carbs: 17.6g; Protein: 53.8g

## 78. Gingered Turkey Meatballs

**Preparation time:** 10 minutes.
**Cooking time:** 10 minutes.
**Servings:** 4
**Ingredients:**

- 1½ pounds ground turkey
- 1 cup shredded cabbage
- ¼ cup chopped fresh cilantro leaves
- 1 tablespoon grated fresh ginger
- 1 teaspoon garlic powder
- 1 teaspoon onion powder
- ½ teaspoon sea salt
- ⅛ teaspoon black pepper
- 2 tablespoons olive oil

**Directions:**

1. In a suitable bowl, combine the turkey, cabbage, cilantro, ginger, garlic powder, onion powder, salt, and pepper. Mix well. Form the turkey mixture into about 20 (¾-inch) meatballs.
2. In a suitable skillet over medium-high heat, heat the olive oil until it shimmers.
3. Add the meatballs and cook for almost 10 minutes, turning as they brown.

**Per serving:** Calories: 270kcal; Fat: 17.2g; Carbs: 2g; Protein: 31.4g

## 79. Chicken Stir-Fry

**Preparation time:** 15 minutes.
**Cooking time:** 15 minutes.
**Servings:** 4
**Ingredients:**

- 3 tablespoons extra-virgin olive oil
- 6 scallions, white and green parts, chopped
- 1 cup broccoli florets
- 1 pound skinless chicken breasts, boneless, diced
- 2 tablespoons toasted sesame seeds

**Directions:**

1. Cut the chicken breast into bite-size pieces.
2. In a suitable skillet over medium-high heat, heat the olive oil until it shimmers.
3. Add the scallions, broccoli, and chicken. Cook for almost 5 to 7 minutes, while stirring occasionally, until the chicken is cooked and the vegetables are tender.
4. Add the stir-fry sauce. Cook for almost 5 minutes, while stirring, until the sauce reduces.
5. Garnish with sesame seeds, if using.

**Per serving:** Calories: 320kcal; Fat: 19g; Carbs: 3.2g; Protein: 33.9g

## 80. Turkey Sweet Potato Hash

**Preparation time:** 10 minutes.
**Cooking time:** 17 minutes.
**Servings:** 4
**Ingredients:**

- 1½ tablespoons avocado oil
- 1 medium yellow onion, peeled and diced
- 2 garlic cloves, minced
- 1 medium sweet potato, cut into cubes (peeling not necessary)
- ½ pound lean ground turkey
- ½ teaspoon salt
- 1 teaspoon Italian seasoning blend

**Directions:**

1. Heat the oil. Allow the oil to heat 1 minute then add the onion and cook until softened, about 5 minutes. Add the garlic then cook for an additional 30 seconds.
2. Add the sweet potato, turkey, salt, and Italian seasoning and cook another 5

minutes. Turn off the heat. Close the lid and secure it well.
3. Pressure cook for 5 minutes.
4. When cooked, release the pressure quickly until the float valve drops and then unlock lid. Spoon onto plates and serve.

**Per serving:** Calories: 146kcal; Fat: 6.6g; Carbs: 10.1g; Protein: 12.4g

## 81. Whole Roasted Chicken

**Preparation time:** 5 minutes.
**Cooking time:** 28 minutes.
**Servings:** 6
**Ingredients:**

- ¾ cup water
- 1 medium lemon
- 1 (4-pound) whole chicken
- 1 tablespoon salt
- 2 teaspoons black pepper

**Directions:**

1. Add water to the inner pot.
2. Cut the lemon in half. Squeeze the juice of half the lemon onto the chicken and sprinkle with black pepper and salt. Stuff the other half of the lemon inside the chicken.
3. Set the chicken in the pot breast side down. Close the lid and secure it well.
4. Pressure cook for 28 minutes.
5. Once cooked, release the presssure naturally then remove the lid.
6. Carefully remove the chicken from your Instant pot and allow it to rest 10 minutes before slicing to serve.

**Per serving:** Calories: 576kcal; Fat: 22.4g; Carbs: 0.5g; Protein: 87.6g

## 82. Easy Chicken And Broccoli

**Preparation time:** 10 minutes.
**Cooking time:** 7 minutes.
**Servings:** 4
**Ingredients:**

- 3 tablespoons extra-virgin olive oil
- 1½ pounds skinless chicken breasts, boneless, diced
- 1½ cups broccoli florets, or chopped broccoli stems
- ½ onion, chopped
- ½ teaspoon sea salt
- ⅛ teaspoon black pepper, freshly ground
- 3 garlic cloves, minced
- 2 cups cooked brown rice

**Directions:**

1. Cut the chicken breasts into bite-size pieces.
2. In a suitable skillet over medium-high heat, heat the olive oil until it shimmers.
3. Add the chicken, broccoli, onion, salt, and pepper. Cook for almost 7 minutes, while stirring occasionally, until the chicken is cooked.
4. Add the garlic. Cook for almost 30 seconds, while stirring constantly.
5. Toss with the brown rice to serve.

**Per serving:** Calories: 389kcal; Fat: 12.9g; Carbs: 38.3g; Protein: 28.8g

## 83. Coconut Lime Chicken With Cauliflower

**Preparation time:** 15 minutes.
**Cooking time:** 11 minutes.
**Servings:** 4
**Ingredients:**

- 1 tablespoon coconut oil
- 1 small yellow onion, peeled and diced
- 2 heaping cups large cauliflower florets
- 1½ pounds chicken breasts, boneless, cut into 1½" chunks

- 1 (13.66-ounce) can full-fat coconut milk, unsweetened
- 1 cup chicken broth
- Juice from 1 medium lime
- 1 teaspoon kosher salt
- 1 teaspoon ground cumin
- ½ teaspoon ground ginger
- 2 cups baby spinach leaves

**Directions:**
1. Heat the oil in your inner pot. When the oil melts, add the onion and cook until it's softened, about 5 minutes.
2. Add the cauliflower, chicken, coconut milk, broth, lime juice, salt, cumin, and ginger and stir well to combine. Close the lid and secure it well.
3. Pressure cook for 6 minutes approximately.
4. Once cooked, release the presssure naturally then remove the lid.
5. Stir in the spinach until it is wilted and then serve.

**Per serving:** Calories: 351kcal; Fat: 20.6g; Carbs: 5.4g; Protein: 35.7g

## 84. Italian Seasoned Turkey Breast

**Preparation time:** 10 minutes.
**Cooking time:** 18 minutes.
**Servings:** 4
**Ingredients:**

- 1½ pounds boneless, turkey breast
- 2 tablespoons avocado oil
- 1 teaspoon sweet paprika
- 1 teaspoon Italian seasoning blend
- ½ teaspoon kosher salt
- ½ teaspoon thyme
- ¼ teaspoon garlic salt
- ¼ teaspoon black pepper

**Directions:**

1. Dry the turkey breast with a towel. Cut the turkey breast in half to fit in your instant pot.
2. Brush both sides of the turkey breast with 1 tablespoon oil.
3. In a suitable bowl, mix together the paprika, Italian seasoning, kosher salt, thyme, garlic salt, and pepper. Rub this mixture onto both sides of the turkey breast.
4. Press the sauté button and heat the rest of the 1 tablespoon oil in your Instant pot 2 minutes. Add the turkey breast and sear it on both sides, about 3 minutes per side. Turn off the heat.
5. Remove the turkey from your Instant pot and place it on a plate. Add 1 cup water to your Instant pot and use a spatula to scrape up any brown bits that are stuck. Set the steam rack in the pot and the turkey breast on top of it. Close the lid and secure it well.
6. Pressure cook for 10 minutes.
7. Once cooked, release the presssure naturally then remove the lid. Slice and serve.

**Per serving:** Calories: 189kcal; Fat: 3.8g; Carbs: 8.1g; Protein: 29.3g

## 85. Chicken Sandwiches With Roasted Red Pepper Aioli

**Preparation time:** 15 minutes.
**Cooking time:** 10 minutes.
**Servings:** 4
**Ingredients:**

- 2 tablespoons extra-virgin olive oil
- 1 pound skinless chicken breasts, boneless, cut into 4 equal pieces and pounded ½ inch thick
- ½ teaspoon sea salt
- ⅛ teaspoon black pepper, freshly ground

- 6 roasted red pepper slices
- ¼ cup anti-inflammatory mayonnaise
- 4 whole-wheat buns

**Directions:**
1. In a suitable skillet over medium-high heat, heat the olive oil until it shimmers.
2. Season the chicken with black pepper and salt. Add it to this skillet and cook for almost 4 minutes per side until the juices run clear.
3. While the chicken cooks, in a suitable blender or food processor, combine the mayonnaise and 2 red pepper pieces. Blend until smooth.
4. Spread the sauce on the buns and top with the rest of the roasted red pepper slices.
5. Top with the chicken.

**Per serving:** Calories: 275kcal; Fat: 15.4g; Carbs: 0g; Protein: 32.8g

## 86. Turkey Kale Fry

**Preparation time:** 10 minutes.
**Cooking time:** 10 minutes.
**Servings:** 4
**Ingredients:**

- 2 tablespoons extra-virgin olive oil
- 1½ pounds ground turkey breast
- 2 cups stemmed and chopped kale
- ½ onion, chopped
- 2 tablespoons fresh thyme leaves
- ½ teaspoon sea salt
- ⅛ teaspoon black pepper
- 5 garlic cloves, minced

**Directions:**
1. In a suitable skillet over medium-high heat, heat the olive oil until it shimmers.
2. Add the turkey, kale, onion, thyme, salt, and pepper. Cook for almost 5 minutes, crumbling the turkey with a spoon until it browns.
3. Add the garlic. Cook for almost 30 seconds, while stirring constantly.

**Per serving:** Calories: 396kcal; Fat: 19.7g; Carbs: 3.4g; Protein: 49.4g

## 87. Ground Turkey And Spinach Stir-Fry

**Preparation time:** 15 minutes.
**Cooking time:** 10 minutes.
**Servings:** 4
**Ingredients:**

- 2 tablespoons extra-virgin olive oil
- 1½ pounds ground turkey breast
- 1 onion, chopped
- 4 cups fresh baby spinach
- 1 recipe stir-fry sauce

**Directions:**
1. In a suitable skillet over medium-high heat, heat the olive oil until it shimmers.
2. Add the turkey, onion, and spinach. Cook for almost 5 minutes, breaking up the turkey with a spoon, until the meat is browned.
3. Add the stir-fry sauce. Cook for almost 3 to 4 minutes, while stirring constantly, until it thickens.

**Per serving:** Calories: 399kcal; Fat: 19.8g; Carbs: 3.7g; Protein: 50g

## 88. Chicken And Cauliflower Bake

**Preparation time:** 5 minutes.
**Cooking time:** 5 minutes.
**Servings:** 4
**Ingredients:**

- 4 cups riced cauliflower
- 8 ounces white mushrooms, chopped
- 8 ounces shiitake mushrooms, stems removed and chopped

- 8 ounces oyster mushrooms, chopped
- 1½ pounds chicken breasts, boneless,, cut into bite-sized pieces
- ¼ cup chicken stock
- 1 tablespoon minced garlic
- 1 teaspoon salt
- 1 teaspoon dried thyme
- Juice from 1 large lemon

**Directions:**
1. Set the cauliflower, mushrooms, and chicken in your Instant Pot.
2. In a suitable bowl, whisk together the stock, garlic, salt, thyme, and lemon juice.
3. Pour the liquid over the ingredients in the instant pot and stir to combine. Close the lid and secure it well.
4. Pressure cook for 5 minutes.
5. Once cooked, release the presssure naturally then remove the lid. Stir and serve.

**Per serving:** Calories: 386kcal; Fat: 3.5g; Carbs: 45.5g; Protein: 41.7g

## 89. Chicken, Mushrooms, And Quinoa

**Preparation time:** 15 minutes.
**Cooking time:** 5 minutes.
**Servings:** 6
**Ingredients:**

- 1 tablespoon avocado oil
- 1 small yellow onion, diced
- 6 garlic cloves, minced
- 1½ pounds boneless, chicken thighs, cut into bite-sized pieces
- 2 (8-ounce) packages sliced white mushrooms
- 3 cups chicken stock
- 1½ cups quinoa, rinsed well
- 1 cup nondairy Greek-style yogurt

**Directions:**
1. Add the oil to your inner pot. Heat the oil for 1 minute. Add the onion and sauté 5 minutes. Add the garlic then sauté for an additional 30 seconds. Turn off the heat.
2. Add the chicken, mushrooms, stock, quinoa, and yogurt and stir to combine. Close the lid and secure it well.
3. Pressure cook for 3 minutes.
4. When cooked, release the pressure quickly until the float valve drops and then unlock lid.
5. Spoon onto plates or into bowls to serve.

**Per serving:** Calories: 434kcal; Fat: 12.3g; Carbs: 35.2g; Protein: 44.2g

## 90. Garlic Turkey Breast

**Preparation time:** 10 minutes.
**Cooking time:** 17 minutes.
**Servings:** 4
**Ingredients:**

- 1 (1½-pound) turkey breast, bonelessand skinless
- 2 tablespoons avocado oil
- Zest from ½ large lemon
- ½ medium shallot, peeled and minced
- 1 large garlic clove, minced
- ½ teaspoon kosher salt
- ¼ teaspoon black pepper

**Directions:**
1. Dry the turkey breast with a towel. Cut the turkey breast in half to fit in your instant pot.
2. Brush both sides of the turkey breast with 1 tablespoon oil.
3. In a suitable bowl, mix together the lemon zest, shallot, garlic, salt, and

pepper. Rub this mixture onto both sides of the turkey breast.

4. Heat the rest of the 1 tablespoon oil in your Instant pot for 2 minutes. Add the turkey breast and sear it on both sides, about 3 minutes per side. Turn off the heat.
5. Remove the turkey from your Instant pot and place it on a plate. Add 1 cup water to your Instant pot and use a spatula to scrape up any brown bits that are stuck. Set the steam rack in the pot and the turkey breast on top of it. Close the lid and secure it well. i
6. Pressure cook for 10 minutes.
7. Once cooked, release the presssure naturally then remove the lid. Slice and serve.

**Per serving:** Calories: 439kcal; Fat: 7.5g; Carbs: 17.8g; Protein: 71.1g

## 91. Lime Chicken And Rice

**Preparation time:** 5 minutes.
**Cooking time:** 5 minutes.
**Servings:** 4
**Ingredients:**

- 1 cup jasmine rice
- 1 (13.66-ounce) can full-fat coconut milk, unsweetened
- ½ cup chicken stock
- 1¼ pounds chicken breasts, boneless,, cut into 1" cubes
- 1 teaspoon salt
- ½ teaspoon ground cumin
- ¼ teaspoon ground ginger
- Juice from 1 medium lime
- ½ cup chopped cilantro leaves and stems

**Directions:**

1. Set the rice, coconut milk, stock, chicken, salt, cumin, and ginger in your Instant pot and stir to combine. Close the lid and secure it well.
2. Pressure cook for 5 minutes.
3. Once cooked, release the presssure naturally then remove the lid.
4. Stir in the lime juice and spoon into four bowls. Top each bowl with an equal amount of cilantro and serve.

**Per serving:** Calories: 532kcal; Fat: 21.5g; Carbs: 31.3g; Protein: 49.6g

## 92. Turkey Burgers

**Preparation time:** 15 minutes.
**Cooking time:** 10 minutes.
**Servings:** 4
**Ingredients:**

- 1 pound ground turkey patties
- ½ teaspoon sea salt
- ⅛ teaspoon black pepper
- 2 tablespoons extra-virgin olive oil
- 1 cup ginger-teriyaki sauce
- 4 pineapple rings

**Directions:**

1. Form the ground turkey breast into 4 patties.
2. Season the turkey burgers with black pepper and salt.
3. In a suitable skillet over medium-high heat, heat the olive oil until it shimmers.
4. Add the burgers and cook for almost 7 minutes, turning once, until cooked through and browned on both sides.
5. While the burgers cook, in a small saucepan over medium-high heat, bring the teriyaki sauce to a simmer, while stirring constantly. Cook for almost 1 to 2 minutes until the sauce thickens.
6. Spoon the warmed sauce over the cooked burgers and top with the pineapple rings.

**Per serving:** Calories: 549kcal; Fat: 30.8g; Carbs: 0g; Protein: 65.1g

### 93. Chicken Bell Pepper Sauté

**Preparation time:** 5 minutes.
**Cooking time:** 15 minutes.
**Servings:** 4
**Ingredients:**

- 3 tablespoons extra-virgin olive oil
- 1 red bell pepper, chopped
- 1 onion, chopped
- 1½ pounds skinless chicken breasts, boneless, diced
- 5 garlic cloves, minced
- ½ teaspoon sea salt
- ¼ teaspoon black pepper, freshly ground

**Directions:**

1. In a suitable skillet over medium-high heat, heat the olive oil until it shimmers.
2. Add the red bell pepper, onion, and chicken. Cook for almost 10 minutes, while stirring it occasionally.
3. Add the garlic, salt, and pepper. Cook for almost 30 seconds, while stirring constantly.

**Per serving:** Calories: 440kcal; Fat: 23.2g; Carbs: 6.1g; Protein: 50.1g

# CHAPTER 5: Meat

### 94. Fried Beef And Bell Pepper

**Preparation time:** 5 minutes
**Cooking time:** 10 minutes
**Servings:** 4
**Ingredients:**

- 1 pound extra-lean ground beef
- 6 scallions, white and green parts, chopped
- 2 red bell peppers, chopped
- 2 tablespoons grated fresh ginger
- ½ teaspoon sea salt
- 3 garlic cloves, minced

**Directions:**

1. In a suitable skillet over medium-high heat, cook the beef for almost 5 minutes, crumbling it with a spoon until it browns.
2. Add the scallions, red bell peppers, ginger, and salt. Cook for almost 4 minutes, while stirring, until the bell peppers are soft.
3. Add the garlic and cook for almost 30 seconds, while stirring constantly.

**Per serving:** Calories: 203kcal; Fat: 6.8g; Carbs: 8.8g; Protein: 26.2g

### 95. Chili-Lime Pork Loin

**Preparation time:** 15 minutes
**Cooking time:** 6-7 hours
**Servings:** 4
**Ingredients:**

- 3 teaspoons chili powder
- 2 teaspoons garlic powder
- 1 teaspoon ground cumin
- ½ teaspoon sea salt
- 2 (1-pound) pork tenderloins
- 1 cup broth
- ¼ cup lime juice

**Directions:**

1. In a suitable bowl, stir together the chili powder, garlic powder, cumin, and salt. Rub the pork all over with the spice mixture, and put it in the slow cooker.
2. Pour the broth and lime juice around the pork in the cooker.
3. Cover the cooker then set to low. Cook for almost 6 to 7 hours.
4. Remove the pork from the slow cooker and let rest for almost 5 minutes. Slice

the pork against the grain into medallions before serving.

**Per serving:** Calories: 478kcal; Fat: 19.2g; Carbs: 2.6g; Protein: 69.5g

## 96. Beef Broth

**Preparation time:** 15 minutes
**Cooking time:** 18-24 hours
**Servings:** 4
**Ingredients:**

- 2 pounds beef marrow bones
- 2 cups chopped onions, celery, carrots, garlic
- 2 bay leaves
- 1 tablespoon apple cider vinegar
- Filtered water, to cover the ingredients

**Directions:**

1. In your slow cooker, combine the bones, onion, celery, carrots, garlic, bay leaves, and vinegar. Add enough water to cover the ingredients.
2. Cover the cooker then set to low. Cook for 18 to 24 hours.
3. Skim off and discard any foam from the surface. Pass the broth through a fine-mesh sieve or cheesecloth into a suitable bowl. Transfer to airtight containers to store.
4. The broth can be kept in refrigerator for almost 3 to 4 days. Freeze any excess for up to 3 months.

**Per serving:** Calories: 96kcal; Fat: 3.6g; Carbs: 5.8g; Protein: 10.4g

## 97. Ground Beef Chili With Tomatoes

**Preparation time:** 10 minutes
**Cooking time:** 15 minutes
**Servings:** 4
**Ingredients:**

- 1 pound extra-lean ground beef
- 1 onion, chopped
- 2 (28-ounce) cans chopped tomatoes, undrained
- 2 (14-ounce) cans kidney beans, drained
- 1 tablespoon chili powder
- 1 teaspoon garlic powder
- ½ teaspoon sea salt

**Directions:**

1. In a suitable pot, cook the beef and onion for almost 5 minutes over medium-high heat, crumbling the beef with a spoon until it browns.
2. Stir in the tomatoes, kidney beans, chili powder, garlic powder, and salt. Bring to a simmer. Cook for almost 10 minutes, while stirring.

**Per serving:** Calories: 564kcal; Fat: 10.1g; Carbs: 64g; Protein: 55.3g

## 98. Pork Ragù

**Preparation time:** 15 minutes
**Cooking time:** 8 hrs.
**Servings:** 4-6
**Ingredients:**

- 1 pound pork tenderloin
- 1 medium yellow onion, diced
- 1 red bell pepper, diced
- 1 (28-ounce) can diced tomatoes
- 2 teaspoons chili powder
- 1 teaspoon garlic powder
- ½ teaspoon ground cumin
- ½ teaspoon smoked paprika
- Dash red pepper flakes
- 1 cup fresh spinach leaves, minced

**Directions:**

1. In your slow cooker, combine the pork, onion, bell pepper, tomatoes, chili powder, garlic powder, cumin, paprika, red pepper flakes, and spinach.

2. Cover the cooker then set to low. Cook for 7 to 8 hours.
3. Transfer the cooked pork loin to a cutting board and shred with a fork. Return it to the slow cooker, stir it into the sauce, and serve.

**Per serving:** Calories: 227kcal; Fat: 4.8g; Carbs: 14g; Protein: 32.4g

## 99. Beefy Lentil Stew

**Preparation time:** 15 minutes
**Cooking time:** 10 minutes
**Servings:** 4
**Ingredients:**

- 2 tablespoons olive oil
- 1 pound extra-lean ground beef
- 1 onion, chopped
- 1 (14-ounce) can lentils, drained
- 1 (14-ounce) can chopped tomatoes with garlic and basil, drained
- ½ teaspoon sea salt
- ⅛ teaspoon black pepper

**Directions:**
1. In your pot, heat the olive oil over medium-high heat until it shimmers.
2. Add the beef and onion, cook them for almost 5 minutes, crumbling the beef with a spoon until it browns.
3. Stir in the lentils, tomatoes, salt, and pepper. Bring to a simmer. Reduce its heat to medium. Cook for almost 3 to 4 minutes, while stirring, until the lentils are hot.

**Per serving:** Calories: 487kcal; Fat: 13.5g; Carbs: 42.6g; Protein: 47.4g

## 100. Beef And Bell Pepper Fajitas

**Preparation time:** 5 minutes
**Cooking time:** 10 minutes
**Servings:** 4
**Ingredients:**

- 3 tablespoons olive oil
- 1½ pounds flank steak, sliced
- 2 green bell peppers, sliced
- 1 onion, sliced
- 1 cup store-bought salsa
- 1 teaspoon garlic powder
- ½ teaspoon sea salt

**Directions:**
1. In a suitable skillet over medium-high heat, heat the olive oil until it shimmers.
2. Add the beef, bell peppers, onion and cook them for almost 6 minutes until the beef browns, stirring occasionally.
3. Stir in the salsa, garlic powder, and salt. Cook for almost 3 minutes, stirring occasionally.

**Per serving:** Calories: 461kcal; Fat: 24.9g; Carbs: 9.6g; Protein: 48.8g

## 101. Beef Meatloaf

**Preparation time:** 15 minutes
**Cooking time:** 5-6 hours
**Servings:** 4
**Ingredients:**

- 1 pound lean ground beef
- 1 small onion, diced
- 1 cup fresh spinach, minced well
- 1 large egg, whisked well
- ½ cup almond milk
- ½ cup sugar-free ketchup
- ½ teaspoon sea salt
- ½ teaspoon garlic powder
- ½ teaspoon dried sage, minced
- ½ teaspoon Dijon mustard

**Directions:**
1. In your slow cooker, mix up the ground beef, onion, spinach, egg, almond milk, ketchup, salt, garlic powder, sage, and mustard. Form the prepared meat mixture into a nice loaf

shape, and position it in the center of your slow cooker.
2. Cover the cooker then set to low. Cook for almost 5 to 6 hours until the center of the meatloaf reaches an internal temperature of 160 degrees F, and then you can serve.

**Per serving:** Calories: 244kcal; Fat: 8.8g; Carbs: 2.6g; Protein: 36.6g

### 102. Fried Beef And Broccoli

**Preparation time:** 10 minutes
**Cooking time:** 10 minutes
**Servings:** 4
**Ingredients:**

- 2 tablespoons olive oil
- 1 pound flank steak, sliced
- 1 cup broccoli florets
- 1 cup sugar snap peas
- 1 zucchini, chopped
- ¼ cup stir-fry sauce

**Directions:**

1. In a suitable skillet, heat the olive oil over medium-high heat until it shimmers.
2. Add the beef and cook for almost 5 to 7 minutes, while stirring occasionally, until it browns. Remove with a slotted spoon then keep it aside on a platter.
3. Add the broccoli, sugar snap peas, and zucchini. Cook for almost 5 minutes, while stirring occasionally, until the vegetables are crisp-tender.
4. Return the beef to this pan. Add the stir-fry sauce. Cook for almost 3 minutes, while stirring, until heated through.

**Per serving:** Calories: 318kcal; Fat: 17.3g; Carbs: 6.7g; Protein: 33.5g

### 103. Hamburgers

**Preparation time:** 10 minutes
**Cooking time:** 10 minutes
**Servings:** 4
**Ingredients:**

- 1 pound extra-lean ground beef patties
- ½ teaspoon sea salt
- ⅛ teaspoon black pepper
- ½ cup garlic aioli
- 3 tablespoons low-; Sodium soy sauce
- 2 tablespoons brown sugar
- 2 tablespoons chopped fresh chives

**Directions:**

1. Season the patties with the black pepper and salt.
2. In a suitable skillet over medium-high heat, cook the patties for almost 5 minutes per side 'til they register an internal temperature of 145 degrees F on an instant-read meat thermometer.
3. While the hamburgers cook, in a suitable bowl, whisk the aioli, soy sauce, brown sugar, and chives.
4. Serve the aioli on top of the hamburgers or anything else that tickles your taste buds.

**Per serving:** Calories: 319kcal; Fat: 11.7g; Carbs: 5.2g; Protein: 45.7g

### 104. Beef Tenderloin

**Preparation time:** 15 minutes
**Cooking time:** 6-7 hours
**Servings:** 4
**Ingredients:**

- 1 pound beef tenderloin, cut into 1-inch chunks
- 1 red bell pepper, seeded and chopped
- 1 yellow bell pepper, seeded and chopped
- 1 green bell pepper, seeded and chopped
- 1 medium onion, chopped
- 1 (14-ounce) can diced tomatoes

- 1 cup beef bone broth or store-bought broth
- ¼ cup coconut aminos
- 1½ teaspoons garlic powder
- 1 teaspoon coconut sugar
- ½ teaspoon ground ginger
- Dash hot sauce
- Black pepper

**Directions:**
1. In your slow cooker, mix and season the beef tenderloin chunks with other ingredients.
2. Cover the cooker and set the cooking temperature to low. Cook for almost 6 to 7 hours and then you can serve.

**Per serving:** Calories: 190kcal; Fat: 7.1g; Carbs: 7.8g; Protein: 23.3g

## 105. Herbed Meatballs

**Preparation time:** 15 minutes
**Cooking time:** 7-8 hours
**Servings:** 6
**Ingredients:**

- 1½ pounds ground beef
- 1 large egg
- 1 small white onion, minced
- ¼ cup minced mushrooms
- 1 teaspoon garlic powder
- ½ teaspoon sea salt
- ½ teaspoon dried oregano
- ¼ teaspoon black pepper
- ¼ teaspoon ground ginger
- Dash red pepper flakes
- 1 (14-ounce) can crushed tomatoes

**Directions:**
1. In a suitable bowl, mix up the ground beef, egg, onion, mushrooms, garlic powder, salt, oregano, black pepper, ginger, and red pepper flakes. Form 12 meatballs from the beef mixture.
2. Pour the tomatoes into the bottom of your slow cooker. Gently arrange the meatballs on top.
3. Cover your slow cooker with its lid. Slow cook for 8 hours and serve.

**Per serving:** Calories: 409kcal; Fat: 13.4g; Carbs: 3.6g; Protein: 64.5g

## 106. Bolognese Sauce

**Preparation time:** 15 minutes
**Cooking time:** 7-8 hours
**Servings:** 4
**Ingredients:**

- 1 tablespoon olive oil
- 3 garlic cloves, minced
- ½ cup chopped onion
- ⅔ cup chopped celery
- ⅔ cup chopped carrot
- 1 pound ground beef
- 1 (14-ounce) can diced tomatoes
- 1 tablespoon white wine vinegar
- ⅛ teaspoon ground nutmeg
- 2 bay leaves
- ½ teaspoon red pepper flakes
- Dash sea salt
- Dash black pepper

**Directions:**
1. Layer the bottom of your slow cooker with the olive oil.
2. Add the garlic, onion, celery, carrot, ground beef, tomatoes, vinegar, nutmeg, bay leaves, red pepper flakes, salt, and black pepper. Using a fork, break up the ground beef as much as possible.
3. Cover your slow cooker with its lid. Slow cook for 7-8 hours.
4. Remove and discard the bay leaves. Stir, breaking up the meat completely, and serve.

**Per serving:** Calories: 186kcal; Fat: 7.2g; Carbs: 5.6g; Protein: 23.9g

### 107. Mustard Pork Tenderloin

**Preparation time:** 10 minutes
**Cooking time:** 15 minutes
**Servings:** 4
**Ingredients:**

- ½ cup fresh parsley leaves
- ¼ cup Dijon mustard
- 6 garlic cloves
- 3 tablespoons fresh rosemary leaves
- 3 tablespoons olive oil
- ½ teaspoon sea salt
- ¼ teaspoon black pepper
- 1 (1½-pound) pork tenderloin

**Directions:**

1. At 400 degrees F, preheat your oven.
2. In a suitable blender, combine the parsley, mustard, garlic, rosemary, olive oil, salt, and pepper. Pulse in 1-second pulses, about 20 times, until a paste forms. Rub this paste all over the tenderloin and put the pork on a rimmed baking sheet.
3. Bake the pork for almost 15 minutes until it registers 165 degrees F on an instant-read meat thermometer.
4. Let rest for almost 5 minutes, slice, and serve.

**Per serving:** Calories: 362kcal; Fat: 17.6g; Carbs: 4.5g; Protein: 45.8g

### 108. Beef Steak Tacos

**Preparation time:** 10 minutes
**Cooking time:** 14 minutes
**Servings:** 4
**Ingredients:**

- ¼ cup fresh cilantro leaves
- 6 tablespoons olive oil
- 4 garlic cloves, minced
- 1 jalapeño pepper, chopped
- 1½ pounds beef flank steak
- ½ teaspoon sea salt
- ⅛ teaspoon black pepper
- Jalapeno guacamole sauce

**Directions:**

1. In a suitable blender or food processor, combine the cilantro, 4 tablespoons of the olive oil, the garlic, and jalapeño. Pulse 10 to 20 (1-second) pulses to make a paste. Set aside 1 tablespoon of the paste and spread the remainder over the flank steak. Let it rest for almost 5 minutes.
2. In a suitable skillet, heat the rest olive oil over medium-high heat until it shimmers.
3. Add the steak and cook the steak for almost 7 minutes on each side until it registers an internal temperature of 125 degrees F.
4. Transfer the cooked steak to a cutting board and let rest for almost 5 minutes. Slice it against the grain into ½-inch-thick slices. Set the slices in a suitable bowl and toss with the reserved 1 tablespoon of herb paste.
5. Serve with the guacamole sauce.

**Per serving:** Calories: 502kcal; Fat: 31.7g; Carbs: 1.2g; Protein: 51.9g

# CHAPTER 6: Snacks and Sides

### 109. Pickled Vegetables

**Preparation time:** 15 minutes.
**Cooking time:** 5 minutes.
**Servings:** 4
**Ingredients:**

- ½ cup cucumber slices
- ½ cup onion slices
- ½ cup carrot slices

- ½ cup red bell pepper strips
- ½ cup apple cider vinegar
- ½ cup water
- 1 ½ teaspoons salt
- 2 teaspoons mustard seeds

**Directions:**
1. Pack cut vegetables tightly into a mason jar.
2. In a small saucepan over high heat, combine vinegar, water, salt, and mustard seeds. Bring to a boil.
3. Pour hot liquid over vegetables. Cap jar and let steep at least 1 hour at room temperature. If not using the same day, put in refrigerator until ready to serve.

**Per serving:** Calories: 30kcal; Fat: 0.5g; Carbs: 4.6g; Protein: 0.8g

### 110. Chickpea Smash

**Preparation time:** 20 minutes.
**Cooking time:** 0 minutes.
**Servings:** 8
**Ingredients:**

- 1 (14-ounce) can chickpeas, drained and rinsed
- ¼ cup lemon juice
- 2 tablespoons chopped fresh parsley
- 3 tablespoons chopped pitted kalamata olives
- ½ teaspoon ground black pepper
- ½ teaspoon salt

**Directions:**
1. In a suitable bowl, using a fork or potato masher, mash chickpeas to the consistency of a chunky paste.
2. Add lemon juice, parsley, olives, pepper, and salt. Mix well and serve.

**Per serving:** Calories: 187kcal; Fat: 3.4g; Carbs: 30.6g; Protein: 9.7g

### 111. Cauliflower Rice With Beans

**Preparation time:** 15 minutes.
**Cooking time:** 20 minutes.
**Servings:** 4
**Ingredients:**

- 2 tablespoons olive oil
- 2 garlic cloves, peeled and minced
- ½ teaspoon ground coriander
- ½ teaspoon ground cumin
- 1 pound (about 4 cups) cauliflower rice
- ½ teaspoon salt
- ½ teaspoon ground black pepper
- 1 (15 ½-ounce) can black beans, drained and rinsed
- 2 tablespoons chopped cilantro
- ¼ cup lime juice

**Directions:**
1. In a large sauté pan over medium-low heat, combine oil, garlic, coriander, and cumin. Sauté 30 seconds, taking care not to brown garlic.
2. Add rice and sauté 10–15 minutes until cauliflower is tender. Season with black pepper and salt.
3. Add beans, cilantro, and lime juice. Cook another 5 minutes until beans are warmed through.

**Per serving:** Calories: 494kcal; Fat: 10.4g; Carbs: 76g; Protein: 27.8g

### 112. Green Smoothie Bowl

**Preparation time:** 5 minutes.
**Cooking time:** 0 minutes.
**Servings:** 2
**Ingredients:**

- ½ cup water
- ¼ cup frozen pineapple cubes
- ¼ cup tightly packed spinach
- ¼ cup ice
- 1 medium pitted date

- 1 medium banana, peeled and sliced in half
- 1 tablespoon hemp seeds

**Directions:**
1. In a suitable blender, purée water, pineapple, spinach, ice, date, and half of banana until smooth and thick.
2. Divide into two bowls. Arrange remaining banana and hemp seeds on top. Serve.

**Per serving:** Calories: 75kcal; Fat: 0.2g; Carbs: 19.4g; Protein: 1g

## 113. Cucumber And Bulgur Salad

**Preparation time:** 15 minutes.
**Cooking time:** 10 minutes.
**Servings:** 4
**Ingredients:**

- ½ cup bulgur
- 1 ½ cups water
- ¾ teaspoon salt
- 2 tablespoons lemon juice
- 3 tablespoons extra-virgin olive oil
- 1 cup medium diced tomato
- 1 cup medium diced cucumber
- ⅓ cup chopped fresh parsley

**Directions:**
1. In a mini saucepan over medium-high heat, combine bulgur, water, and ¼ teaspoon salt. Bring to a boil. Then cover, reduce heat to simmer, and cook 10 minutes. Turn off heat and let sit, covered, another 5 minutes.
2. Drain off any excess liquid, fluff bulgur with a fork, and place in a serving bowl, letting it come to room temperature while preparing rest of salad.
3. In a suitable bowl, whisk together lemon juice, oil, and remaining ½ teaspoon salt.
4. Add tomato, cucumber, and parsley to the bowl with bulgur. Add dressing, toss well to combine, then serve.

**Per serving:** Calories: 164kcal; Fat: 10.9g; Carbs: 16g; Protein: 2.8g

## 114. Yogurt With Dates

**Preparation time:** 5 minutes.
**Cooking time:** 0 minutes.
**Servings:** 4
**Ingredients:**

- 2 cups coconut yogurt, unsweetened
- ¼ cup chopped almonds
- ¼ cup chopped walnuts
- 2 pitted dates, chopped
- ½ teaspoon ground cinnamon

**Directions:**
1. In a suitable bowl, stir together the yogurt, almonds, walnuts, dates, and cinnamon. Serve immediately.

**Per serving:** Calories: 161kcal; Fat: 10.7g; Carbs: 11.8g; Protein: 6.3g

## 115. Zucchini Fritters

**Preparation time:** 20 minutes.
**Cooking time:** 20 minutes.
**Servings:** 4
**Ingredients:**

- ¼ cup sriracha sauce
- 1 cup plain, whole milk Greek yogurt
- 1 cup shredded zucchini
- 1 cup chickpeas, mashed well
- 1 cup fresh corn kernels
- 3 large eggs, whisked
- 1 cup almond meal
- ¼ cup chopped fresh parsley
- 1 teaspoon salt
- ½ teaspoon ground black pepper

- ½ teaspoon turmeric
- ¼ cup avocado oil

**Directions:**
1. In a suitable bowl, whisk together sriracha and yogurt. Set aside to serve with fritters.
2. In a suitable bowl, combine zucchini, chickpeas, corn, eggs, almond meal, parsley, salt, pepper, and turmeric.
3. In your medium sauté pan over medium heat, heat 1 tablespoon oil, taking care not to let it smoke. Scoop about 2 tablespoons batter for each fritter onto pan into round disks.
4. Cook on both sides for almost 3 minutes or until golden brown. Repeat with remaining batter, adding oil as necessary.
5. Serve fritters hot or at room temperature with dipping sauce.

**Per serving:** Calories: 470kcal; Fat: 22g; Carbs: 47.3g; Protein: 26.3g

### 116. Pickled Shiitake

**Preparation time:** 10 minutes.
**Cooking time:** 15 minutes.
**Servings:** 8
**Ingredients:**

- 2 cups dried shiitake mushroom caps
- ¼ cup tamari
- ¼ cup brown rice vinegar
- 2 tablespoons pure maple syrup
- 1 2" piece fresh ginger, peeled and cut into thin slices

**Directions:**
1. Put mushrooms in a small saucepan and cover with boiling water. Let them soak about 30 minutes. Drain mushrooms, reserving 1 cup soaking liquid.
2. Slice rehydrated mushrooms into ¼" slices.
3. Return mushrooms and reserved soaking liquid to saucepan and add tamari, vinegar, maple syrup, and ginger. Simmer 15 minutes over low heat.
4. Remove it from the heat and cool to room temperature. Store in an airtight container (along with liquid). Eat immediately or keep refrigerated up to two weeks.

**Per serving:** Calories: 153kcal; Fat: 0.4g; Carbs: 34.3g; Protein: 2.3g

### 117. Bean Salsa

**Preparation time:** 20 minutes.
**Cooking time:** 30 minutes.
**Servings:** 6
**Ingredients:**

- 1 cup dried pinto beans, rinsed
- 3 cups vegetable broth
- 1 teaspoon sea salt
- 1 red onion, chopped
- 1 cup fresh cilantro, chopped
- 1 cup chopped tomatoes
- 1 avocado, peeled, halved, pitted, and diced
- 1 small jalapeño pepper, seeded and minced
- 1 cup frozen corn
- Juice of 1 lime
- Organic blue corn chips, for serving

**Directions:**
1. In the instant pot, combine the beans, broth, and salt. Lock the lid.
2. Presssure cook at high for almost 30 minutes.
3. While the beans cook, in a suitable bowl, stir together the red onion, cilantro, tomatoes, avocado, and jalapeño. Set aside.

4. When cooking is complete, use a natural release.
5. Remove the lid then stir in the frozen corn. Transfer the bean mixture to the bowl with the tomato and cilantro mixture, add the lime juice, and stir to combine well. Serve with the corn chips.

**Per serving:** Calories: 235kcal; Fat: 8g; Carbs: 31.3g; Protein: 11.3g

## 118. Maple Collard Greens

**Preparation time:** 15 minutes.
**Cooking time:** 40 minutes.
**Servings:** 4
**Ingredients:**

- 2 tablespoons extra-virgin olive oil
- 1 cup small diced yellow onion
- 2 garlic cloves, peeled and minced
- 1 bunch collard greens, hard stems removed and cut into 1" strips
- 1 ½ cups water
- 3 tablespoons apple cider vinegar
- ¼ teaspoon salt
- ¼ teaspoon ground black pepper
- 1 teaspoon ground coriander
- 1 tablespoon pure maple syrup
- ¼ teaspoon red pepper flakes

**Directions:**

1. In a large sauté pan over low heat, warm oil. Add onions and cook 7 minutes until they are tender and transparent.
2. Add garlic and sauté 30 seconds, just until fragrant.
3. Add collards and water to pan. After 1 minute, once greens have wilted down a bit, add remaining ingredients to pan.
4. Cover with a lid and cook 30 minutes. Check on greens every 5 minutes. If they look dry, add water, 1 cup at a time. It's important that they are cooking in liquid throughout. Serve hot.

**Per serving:** Calories: 96kcal; Fat: 7.2g; Carbs: 8.3g; Protein: 0.9g

## 119. Toasted Nut Mix

**Preparation time:** 5 minutes.
**Cooking time:** 6 minutes approximately.
**Servings:** 6
**Ingredients:**

- 1 cup raw cashews
- 1 cup raw almonds
- 1 teaspoon ghee
- ¼ teaspoon curry powder
- ¼ teaspoon garlic powder
- ¼ teaspoon sea salt

**Directions:**

1. Layer a plate with a paper towel and set aside.
2. Select sauté on the instant pot and let the pot preheat.
3. In the pot, combine the cashews and almonds. Toast for almost 6 minutes, while stirring frequently to keep the nuts from burning, until they begin to brown lightly.
4. Add the ghee, curry powder, garlic powder, and salt, mixing well until the nuts are thoroughly coated. Transfer the seasoned nuts to the prepared plate to cool. The cashews will be slightly chewy when warm.
5. Store in an airtight container in a cool dark cabinet for up to 5 days.

**Per serving:** Calories: 172kcal; Fat: 14.4g; Carbs: 8.3g; Protein: 5.2g

## 120. Flaxseed Power Bites

**Preparation time:** 20 minutes.
**Cooking time:** 0 minutes.
**Servings:** 1

**Ingredients:**

- 1 cup almond butter, unsweetened
- ½ cup ground flaxseed
- ¼ cup almond or coconut flour
- ¼ cup cocoa powder, unsweetened
- ¼ cup coconut flakes, unsweetened
- ¼ cup roasted pumpkin seeds
- ¼ cup chia seeds
- 1 teaspoon ground cinnamon
- 1 to 2 teaspoons monk fruit extract

**Directions:**

1. In a suitable bowl, combine the almond butter, flaxseed, almond flour, cocoa powder, coconut flakes, pumpkin seeds, chia seeds, cinnamon, and monk fruit extract.
2. Using your hands, mix everything together and shape the prepared mixture into 12 (1-inch) balls. Place them in a single layer on your baking sheet or in a large container. Cover and refrigerate for at least 1 hour before serving.
3. Store the balls in your airtight container in the refrigerator for up to one week or in your freezer for up to three months.

**Per serving:** Calories: 251kcal; Fat: 19.7g; Carbs: 11.7g; Protein: 10.7g

### 121. Brussels Sprouts With Walnuts

**Preparation time:** 15 minutes.
**Cooking time:** 11 minutes.
**Servings:** 4
**Ingredients:**

- 1½ pounds Brussels sprouts
- ¼ cup ghee
- 3 garlic cloves, minced
- ½ teaspoon sea salt
- ¼ teaspoon black pepper
- 1 cup vegetable broth
- 1 tablespoon Dijon mustard
- ½ cup raw walnuts, chopped

**Directions:**

1. Select sauté on your instant pot and let the pot preheat.
2. Set the brussels sprouts in the pot and add the ghee, garlic, salt, and pepper. Cook for almost 6 minutes approximately.
3. Stir in the broth and mustard, mixing well to combine. Turn off heat. Lock the lid.
4. Pressure cook at high for almost 5 minutes.
5. When cooking is complete, use a quick release. Remove the lid.
6. Sprinkle the Brussels sprouts with the walnuts and serve.

**Per serving:** Calories: 298kcal; Fat: 23.1g; Carbs: 18.3g; Protein: 11.1g

### 122. Sweet Potato Mash

**Preparation time:** 10 minutes.
**Cooking time:** 25 minutes.
**Servings:** 4
**Ingredients:**

- 1 cup water
- 4 large (8- to 12-ounce) sweet potatoes, pierced with a fork multiple times
- 1 teaspoon ghee
- ½ teaspoon sea salt, more for garnish
- ¼ teaspoon ground nutmeg
- ½ cup chopped walnuts
- ½ cup nondairy milk (such as coconut milk)
- Freshly grated nutmeg, for garnish

**Directions:**

1. Place a metal trivet or steam rack in the instant pot and pour in the water.

Set the sweet potatoes on the trivet. Lock the lid.
2. Select pressure cook and cook at high pressure for almost 25 minutes. To ensure the sweet potatoes cook evenly, make sure they are all the same size.
3. While the sweet potatoes cook, in a suitable bowl, stir together the ghee, salt, nutmeg, walnuts, and milk. Set aside.
4. When cooking is complete, use a natural release for almost 10 minutes, then quick release any remaining pressure.
5. Remove the lid. Using potholders, remove the trivet and place it in a clean sink or on a cutting board to cool.
6. Gently pull off the skins from the cooked sweet potatoes and discard them. Add the sweet potato flesh to the prepared mixture in the bowl. Using your large spoon or potato masher, mash the ingredients until combined. Garnish with sea salt or nutmeg.

**Per serving:** Calories: 299kcal; Fat: 11.2g; Carbs: 44.9g; Protein: 7.1g

## 123. Cinnamon Applesauce

**Preparation time:** 15 minutes.
**Cooking time:** 8 minutes.
**Servings:** 6
**Ingredients:**

- 8 honey crisp apples, peeled, cored, and chopped
- 1 cup water
- ½ teaspoon ground cinnamon

**Directions:**
1. In the instant pot, combine the apples, water, and cinnamon. Lock the lid.
2. Pressure cook at high for 8 minutes.
3. When cooking is complete, use a quick release. Remove the lid.
4. Pour the cooked apples into a high-powered blender and blend until smooth.
5. Refrigerate in mason jars for up to 10 days.

**Per serving:** Calories: 155kcal; Fat: 0.5g; Carbs: 41.2g; Protein: 0.8g

## 124. Pico De Gallo

**Preparation time:** 5 minutes.
**Cooking time:** 0 minutes.
**Servings:** 4
**Ingredients:**

- 2 large ripe tomatoes, diced
- ¼ cup chopped onion
- ¼ cup small diced green bell pepper
- ¼ cup chopped fresh cilantro
- 2 tablespoons lime juice
- ¾ teaspoon salt
- ⅛ teaspoon cayenne pepper

**Directions:**
1. In a suitable bowl, combine all the recipe ingredients and mix well.
2. Taste and adjust seasonings if necessary.

**Per serving:** Calories: 21kcal; Fat: 0.2g; Carbs: 4.6g; Protein: 1g

## 125. Fennel Cabbage Slaw

**Preparation time:** 25 minutes.
**Cooking time:** 0 minutes.
**Servings:** 6
**Ingredients:**

- 2 cups shredded red cabbage
- 1 teaspoon salt
- 1 tablespoon orange juice
- 2 tablespoons lime juice
- 2 teaspoons rice wine vinegar
- 3 tablespoons extra-virgin olive oil
- 1 tablespoon raw honey

- 1 medium carrot, grated (about ½ cup)
- 1 medium bulb fennel, sliced (about 1 cup)
- ¼ cup chopped fresh cilantro
- ½ cup toasted pumpkin seeds

**Directions:**
1. In a suitable bowl, place cabbage and ½ teaspoon salt. Massage with your hands for almost 3–4 minutes. Leave to rest.
2. In a suitable bowl, whisk orange juice, lime juice, vinegar, oil, honey, and remaining salt.
3. To the bowl with cabbage, add carrots, fennel, cilantro, pumpkin seeds, and dressing. Mix well. Serve.

**Per serving:** Calories: 150kcal; Fat: 12.3g; Carbs: 8.6g; Protein: 3.4g

### 126. Citrus Spinach

**Preparation time:** 10 minutes
**Cooking time:** 7 minutes
**Servings:** 4
**Ingredients:**

- 2 tablespoons extra-virgin olive oil
- 4 cups fresh baby spinach
- 2 garlic cloves, minced
- Juice of ½ orange
- Zest of ½ orange
- ½ teaspoon sea salt
- ⅛ teaspoon black pepper

**Directions:**
1. In a suitable skillet over medium-high heat, heat the olive oil until it shimmers.
2. Toss in the spinach and cook for 3 minutes, stirring occasionally.
3. Add the garlic. Cook for 30 seconds, stirring constantly.
4. Add the orange juice, orange zest, salt, and pepper. Cook for almost 2 minutes, constantly stirring, until the juice evaporates.

**Per serving:** Calories: 117kcal; Fat: 7.1g; Carbs: 12.8g; Protein: 5g

# CHAPTER 7: Dessert

### 127. Peach-Raspberry Crumble

**Preparation time:** 20 minutes
**Cooking time:** 40 minutes
**Servings:** 10
**Ingredients:**

- 5 medium fresh peaches, peeled and cut into ¼" slices
- 1 pint fresh raspberries
- ½ cup pure maple syrup
- ¾ cup 1 tablespoon whole-wheat pastry flour
- ½ cup rolled oats (not instant)
- ½ cup chopped pecans
- ¼ teaspoon salt
- 5 tablespoons olive oil

**Directions:**
1. At 350 degrees F, preheat your oven.
2. In a suitable bowl, combine peaches, raspberries, ¼ cup of maple syrup, and 1 tablespoon flour and mix well. Pour fruit mixture into a 9" round baking pan and set aside.
3. In a suitable bowl, combine the remaining ¾ cup flour, oats, pecans, and salt and mix well. Add theremaining ¼ cup maple syrup and oil. Gently mix until flour and oats are evenly moist. Toward end of mixing, your fingers can be used to press mixture into different-sized

crumbles—some will be fine and other parts will be larger clumps.
4. Pour crumble topping loosely over fruit, covering evenly.
5. Bake 40 minutes until crumble top is golden brown and fruit has bubbled up.
6. Remove from your oven and let cool at least 30 minutes before serving.

**Per serving:** Calories: 213kcal; Fat: 12.1g; Carbs: 26.5g; Protein: 2.4g

### 128. Ginger Jam Dots

**Preparation time:** 5 minutes
**Cooking time:** 0 minutes
**Servings:** 12
**Ingredients:**

- ¼ cup melted coconut oil
- 3 tablespoons pure maple syrup
- ½ teaspoon vanilla extract
- 2 cups almond flour
- 1 teaspoon ground cinnamon
- ⅛ teaspoon salt
- ⅓ cup berry ginger jam

**Directions:**

1. At 325 degrees F, preheat your oven. Layer a baking sheet with parchment paper.
2. In a suitable bowl, combine oil, maple syrup, and vanilla. Add flour, cinnamon, and salt. Stir into a thick batter.
3. Roll cookies into ¾" balls. Place on baking sheet 1"–1 ½" apart. Flatten slightly into a disk shape. Using thumb, press an indentation into middle of each cookie. Place about 1 teaspoon jam into each indentation.
4. Bake 12–15 minutes until cookies are golden brown. Remove from oven and cool. Cookies will firm up once completely cool.

**Per serving:** Calories: 124kcal; Fat: 6.8g; Carbs: 15.4g; Protein: 1.1g

### 129. Almond Butter Mini Muffins

**Preparation time:** 10 minutes
**Cooking time:** 5 minutes
**Servings:** 9
**Ingredients:**

- 6 ounces dark chocolate, chopped
- ½ cup natural almond butter
- 2 tablespoons raw honey
- ½ teaspoon vanilla extract
- Sea salt, to taste

**Directions:**

1. Layer a 9-cup muffin tin with paper muffin cups.
2. Melt the chocolate in a saucepan over low heat, then divide half of the chocolate in the muffin cups. Set the rest of the half aside.
3. In a suitable bowl, mix up the almond butter, vanilla and honey. Divide and shape the prepared mixture into 9 balls, then drop each ball in each muffin cup.
4. Top the balls with remaining melted chocolate, then sprinkle with salt.
5. Set the muffin tin in the refrigerator for at least 3 hours or until solid.
6. Serve chilled.

**Per serving:** Calories: 255kcal; Fat: 17.9g; Carbs: 16.6g; Protein: 7.1g

### 130. Apple Cinnamon Muesli

**Preparation time:** 10 minutes
**Cooking time:** 0 minutes
**Servings:** 4 to 6
**Ingredients:**

- 2 cups rolled oats
- ¼ cup no-added-sugar apple juice
- 1¾ cups coconut milk
- 1 tablespoon apple cider vinegar

- 1 apple, cored and chopped
- Dash ground cinnamon

**Directions:**
1. In a suitable bowl, mix up the oats, apple juice, coconut milk, and apple cider vinegar. Wrap the bowl in plastic and refrigerate the mixture overnight.
2. Remove the bowl from the refrigerator. Top with apple and sprinkle with cinnamon, then serve.

**Per serving:** Calories: 384kcal; Fat: 32.2g; Carbs: 24.2g; Protein: 5.4g

### 131. Almond-Orange Torte

**Preparation time:** 45 minutes
**Cooking time:** 1 hr. 30 minutes
**Servings:** 16
**Ingredients:**

- 3 large oranges
- 2 bay leaves
- 1 cinnamon stick
- ¾ cup sucanat
- 6 large eggs
- ½ teaspoon baking powder
- 3 ½ cups almond meal
- 1 cup hazelnut meal
- ¾ cup dark chocolate chips (cacao or higher)

**Directions:**
1. At 350 degrees F, preheat your oven grease and flour a 9" × 13" pan.
2. In a medium pot, combine oranges, bay leaves, and cinnamon and cover with water. Bring to a boil and simmer over low heat 45 minutes until oranges are easily pierced with a fork. Cut them in quarters and let cool. Take out seeds and blend in a food processor until mash is chunky but even.
3. In a suitable bowl, combine orange purée, sucanat, eggs, baking powder, and nut meals. Mix well, then fold in chocolate chips.
4. Pour batter into prepared cake pan. Bake the food for 40–45 minutes.
5. Let cool at least 30 minutes before serving.

**Per serving:** Calories: 220kcal; Fat: 16.6g; Carbs: 13.4g; Protein: 8.2g

### 132. Blueberry Cobbler

**Preparation time:** 15 minutes
**Cooking time:** 2 hours
**Servings:** 4 to 6
**Ingredients:**

- 3 tablespoons coconut oil
- 2 cups frozen blueberries
- 3 large peaches, peeled and sliced
- 1 cup rolled oats
- 1 cup almond flour
- 1 tablespoon coconut sugar
- ½ teaspoon vanilla extract
- 1 tablespoon pure maple syrup
- 1 teaspoon ground cinnamon
- Pinch ground nutmeg

**Directions:**
1. Grease the slow cooker with 1 tablespoon of coconut oil.
2. Put the blueberries and peaches in the single layer in the slow cooker.
3. In a suitable bowl, mix up the rest of the ingredients. Break the prepared mixture into chunks with your hands, then spread the chunks on top of the blueberries and peaches in the slow cooker.
4. Cover the slow cooker lid and cook on high for almost 2 hours or until golden brown.
5. Allow to cool for almost 15 minutes, then serve warm.

**Per serving:** Calories: 300kcal; Fat: 16.9g; Carbs: 32.5g; Protein: 6.9g

## 133. Chai Pudding

**Preparation time:** 5 minutes
**Cooking time:** 0 minutes
**Servings:** 2
**Ingredients:**

- ½ cup 2 tablespoons canned coconut milk
- ½ teaspoon sweet spice blend
- 1 teaspoon pure maple syrup
- 2 tablespoons chia seeds

**Directions:**

1. In your small pot, over low heat, warm milk just until it achieves a liquid and uniform consistency.
2. In a suitable bowl or mason jar, combine milk, sweet spice blend, maple syrup, and chia seeds. Stir well to combine. Place in refrigerator with a tight-fitting lid for at least 2 hours.
3. Remove from refrigerator and eat as is.

**Per serving:** Calories: 284kcal; Fat: 23g; Carbs: 17.5g; Protein: 6.1g

## 134. Spice Stuffed Apple Bake

**Preparation time:** 15 minutes
**Cooking time:** 2 hours
**Servings:** 5 apples
**Ingredients:**

- 5 apples, cored
- ½ cup water
- ½ cup crushed pecans
- ¼ teaspoon ground cloves
- 1 teaspoon ground cinnamon
- ¼ teaspoon ground cardamom
- ½ teaspoon ground ginger
- ¼ cup melted coconut oil

**Directions:**

1. Peel a thin strip off the top of each apple.
2. Pour the water in the slow cooker, then arrange the apples in the slow cooker, upright.
3. In a suitable bowl, mix up the rest of the ingredients in a suitable bowl.
4. Spread the prepared mixture on tops of the apples, then put the slow cooker lid on and cook on high for almost 2 hours or until the apples are tender.
5. Allow to cool for almost 15 minutes, then remove the apples from the slow cooker gently and serve warm.

**Per serving:** Calories: 292kcal; Fat: 19.3g; Carbs: 33g; Protein: 1.9g

## 135. Banana Cacao Brownies

**Preparation time:** 15 minutes
**Cooking time:** 3 hours
**Servings:** 4 to 6
**Ingredients:**

- 3 tablespoons coconut oil
- 2 ripe bananas, mashed
- 1 cup cacao powder
- 1 cup almond butter
- 2 large eggs
- ½ cup coconut sugar
- 2 teaspoons vanilla extract
- 1 teaspoon baking soda
- ½ teaspoon sea salt

**Directions:**

1. Grease the slow cooker with 1 tablespoon of coconut oil.
2. In a suitable bowl, mix up the rest of the ingredients until a batter forms.
3. Pour the batter in the greased slow cooker. Cover and cook on low for almost 3 hours or until lightly firmed and a toothpick inserted in the center comes out clean.

4. Remove the brownies from the slow cooker and slice to serve.

**Per serving:** Calories: 181kcal; Fat: 12.8g; Carbs: 19.1g; Protein: 5.8g

## 136. Coconut Hot Chocolate

**Preparation time:** 5 minutes
**Cooking time:** 7 minutes
**Servings:** 2
**Ingredients:**

- 1 tablespoon coconut oil
- 2 cups coconut milk
- 1 tablespoon collagen protein powder
- 2 tablespoons cocoa powder
- 2 teaspoons coconut sugar
- ½ teaspoon ground turmeric
- 1 teaspoon ground ginger
- 1 teaspoon vanilla extract
- 1 teaspoon ground cinnamon
- Sea salt, to taste
- Cayenne pepper, to taste

**Directions:**

1. Heat the coconut oil and almond milk in a saucepan over medium heat for 7 minutes. Stir constantly.
2. Mix in the collagen protein powder, then fold in the cocoa powder and coconut sugar. Stir to mix well.
3. Pour the prepared mixture in a suitable blender, then add the rest of the ingredients. Pulse until the prepared mixture is creamy and bubbly.
4. Serve immediately.

**Per serving:** Calories: 559kcal; Fat: 55.8g; Carbs: 15.5g; Protein: 9.2g

## 137. Quinoa With Raspberries

**Preparation time:** 10 minutes
**Cooking time:** 20 minutes
**Servings:** 4
**Ingredients:**

- 1 cup quinoa, rinsed
- 2 cups water
- ¼ cup hemp seeds
- ½ cup shredded coconut
- 1 teaspoon ground cinnamon
- 2 tablespoons flaxseeds
- 1 teaspoon vanilla extract
- Pinch sea salt
- ¼ cup chopped hazelnuts
- 1 cup fresh raspberries

**Directions:**

1. In your saucepan, pour in the quinoa and water. Bring to a boil over high heat. Reduce its heat to low and simmer for almost 20 minutes or until soft.
2. When the simmering is complete, mix in the hemp seeds, coconut, cinnamon, flaxseeds, vanilla, and salt.
3. Serve the quinoa with hazelnuts and raspberries on top.

**Per serving:** Calories: 302kcal; Fat: 13.5g; Carbs: 35.3g; Protein: 10.6g

## 138. Chia Pudding With Cherries

**Preparation time:** 10 minutes
**Cooking time:** 0 minutes
**Servings:** 4
**Ingredients:**

- 2 cups almond milk
- ½ cup chia seeds
- 1 teaspoon vanilla extract
- ¼ cup pure maple syrup
- ½ cup chopped cashews
- 1 cup frozen no-added-sugar pitted cherries, thawed, juice reserved

**Directions:**

1. In a suitable bowl, mix up the almond milk, chia seeds, vanilla, and maple

syrup. Refrigerate the mixture overnight.
2. Divide the almond milk mixture in four bowls, then serve with cashews and cherries on top.

**Per serving:** Calories: 340kcal; Fat: 27.3g; Carbs: 22.9g; Protein: 5.3g

### 139. Brownies With Strawberry Sauce

**Preparation time:** 10 minutes
**Cooking time:** 20 minutes
**Servings:** 9 brownies
**Ingredients:**

- For the strawberry sauce:
- 1 cup mashed fresh strawberries
- 2 teaspoons coconut sugar
- 1 tablespoon filtered water
- For the banana brownies:
- Coconut oil, for greasing this pan
- ½ cup cocoa powder
- ¼ cup coconut sugar
- ¾ cup almond butter
- 1 egg yolk, whisked
- 1 teaspoon vanilla extract
- ½ teaspoon baking soda
- 1 ripe banana, mashed
- ¼ teaspoon sea salt

**Directions:**

1. To make the strawberry sauce:
2. Put the ingredients for the strawberry sauce in a saucepan and heat them for 6 minutes or until thickened and well combined, stirring instantly.
3. Turn off the heat and set aside until ready to use.
4. To make the banana brownies:
5. At 350 degrees F, preheat your oven. Grease a baking pan with coconut oil.
6. Combine the cocoa powder, coconut sugar, and almond butter in a suitable bowl. Stir to mix well.
7. Combine the egg yolk, vanilla, baking soda, banana, and salt in a separate bowl. Stir to mix well.
8. Make a will in the center of the cocoa powder mixture, then pour the prepared egg mixture in the well. Stir to mix well until a batter forms.
9. Pour the batter in the prepared baking pan, then level with a spatula.
10. Bake in the preheated oven for almost 12 minutes or until a toothpick inserted in the center comes out clean.
11. Remove the brownies from your oven and allow to cool for almost 5 minutes.
12. Glaze the brownies with strawberry sauce and slice to serve.

**Per serving:** Calories: 118kcal; Fat: 5.6g; Carbs: 19.4g; Protein: 3.8g

### 140. Berry Pops

**Preparation time:** 5 minutes
**Cooking time:** 0 minutes
**Servings:** 4
**Ingredients:**

- 1 cup blueberries, fresh or frozen
- 1 cup strawberries, fresh or frozen
- 2 tablespoons raw honey
- 2 cups plain whole-milk yogurt
- 1 teaspoon lemon juice
- ¼ cup filtered water

**Directions:**

1. In your blender, add all the ingredients, then pulse to combine well until creamy and smooth.
2. Pour the prepared mixture in the ice pop molds, then place in the freezer to free for at least 3 hours. Serve chilled.

**Per serving:** Calories: 120kcal; Fat: 0.3g; Carbs: 26.4g; Protein: 3.1g

### 141. Banana Pops

**Preparation time:** 15 minutes

**Cooking time:** 0 minutes
**Servings:** 4
**Ingredients:**

- ¼ cup dark chocolate chips (cacao or higher)
- 2 large ripe bananas
- 4 popsicle sticks
- ½ cup plain, whole milk Greek yogurt
- ½ cup anti-inflammatory granola, crushed into small chunks

**Directions:**

1. Prepare your baking sheet with parchment paper. Be sure tray will fit in a freezer.
2. Fill a medium saucepan ⅓ of the way with water. Place a suitable bowl on top of it. It should fit securely, but bottom of bowl should not touch bottom of pot. Place chocolate in bowl and melt, while stirring occasionally.
3. Peel bananas and cut them in half crosswise. Insert sticks into cut ends of bananas.
4. Place yogurt in a small shallow bowl.
5. Place granola on a flat plate.
6. To assemble, dip and roll banana in yogurt. Spread with back of a spoon or pastry brush to make sure it is well coated. Then roll banana in granola until it is evenly coated. Use your fingers to gently help granola stick.
7. Place banana pops on sheet and drizzle melted chocolate evenly over them.
8. Place tray in freezer at least 2 hours or up to overnight to firm up toppings. Serve.

**Per serving:** Calories: 179kcal; Fat: 11.9g; Carbs: 41.9g; Protein: 7.9g

### 142. Chocolate Tofu Pudding

**Preparation time:** 15 minutes
**Cooking time:** 0 minutes
**Servings:** 8
**Ingredients:**

- 2 cups dark chocolate chips (cacao or higher)
- 1 pound silken tofu
- 1 teaspoon vanilla extract

**Directions:**

1. Fill a medium saucepan ⅓ of the way with water. Place a suitable bowl on top. It should fit securely, but bottom of bowl should not touch bottom of pot. Place chocolate in bowl and melt, while stirring occasionally. (a double boiler may be used or you can melt chocolate in the microwave.)
2. In your blender, add tofu, melted chocolate, vanilla and then blend until smooth.
3. Pour into your glass container, cover, and refrigerate at least 1 hour. Serve.

**Per serving:** Calories: 177kcal; Fat: 9.5g; Carbs: 21.4g; Protein: 5.9g

### 143. Strawberry Granita

**Preparation time:** 20 minutes
**Cooking time:** 0 minutes
**Servings:** 8
**Ingredients:**

- 4 cups hot water
- 2 medium pitted dates
- 2 white tea bags (decaffeinated if children under twelve years old are served)
- 2 cups strawberries

**Directions:**

1. Place hot water in a suitable bowl or pitcher. Add dates and tea bags. Steep 20 minutes.
2. Remove tea bags. Cool.
3. Pour cooled tea and dates into blender. Add strawberries. Blend until smooth.

4. Pour blended mixture into a large glass casserole dish and place in freezer for almost 2 hours. (if frozen for much longer than that, it becomes harder to scrape.)
5. Remove from freezer and scrape thoroughly with a fork into small ice crystals. If bottom layers are not yet frozen enough to scrape, return to freezer for another hour and repeat scraping.
6. Serve in parfait cups.

**Per serving:** Calories: 17kcal; Fat: 0.1g; Carbs: 4.3g; Protein: 0.3g

## 144. Chocolate Bark

**Preparation time:** 10 minutes
**Cooking time:** 5 minutes
**Servings:** 8
**Ingredients:**

- 2 cups dark chocolate chips (cacao or higher)
- ½ cup chopped dried figs
- ½ cup chopped pecans
- ½ teaspoon orange zest
- ½ teaspoon fennel seeds, crushed or chopped

**Directions:**
1. Layer a cookie sheet with parchment paper.
2. Fill a medium saucepan ⅓ of the way with water. Place a suitable bowl on top. It should fit securely, but bottom of bowl should not touch bottom of pot. Place chocolate chips in bowl and melt, while stirring occasionally. (you can melt chocolate in the microwave.)
3. Once chocolate is smooth and melted, pour it onto cookie sheet. Spread with a spatula into a thin, even layer.
4. Sprinkle evenly with figs, pecans, orange zest, and fennel seeds, and place in refrigerator to set at least 2 hours or overnight.
5. Once set, break into pieces and serve.

**Per serving:** Calories: 220kcal; Fat: 13.1g; Carbs: 29.1g; Protein: 3.2g

## 145. Glazed Pears With Hazelnuts

**Preparation time:** 10 minutes
**Cooking time:** 15 minutes
**Servings:** 4
**Ingredients:**

- 4 pears, peeled, cored, and quartered lengthwise
- 1 cup apple juice
- 1 tablespoon grated fresh ginger
- ½ cup pure maple syrup
- ¼ cup chopped hazelnuts

**Directions:**
1. Put the pears in a suitable pot, then pour the apple juice over. Bring to a boil over medium-high heat.
2. Reduce its heat to medium-low, then cover and simmer for almost 15 minutes or until the pears are tender.
3. Meanwhile, put the ginger and maple syrup in a saucepan. Bring to a boil over medium-high heat. Stir constantly. Turn off the heat then let stand until ready to use.
4. Transfer the simmered pears onto a large plate, then glaze with the gingered maple syrup. Spread the hazelnuts on top and serve warm.

**Per serving:** Calories: 286kcal; Fat: 3.4g; Carbs: 67g; Protein: 1.6g

## 146. Mango-Peach Yogurt

**Preparation time:** 15 minutes
**Cooking time:** 0 minutes
**Servings:** 6
**Ingredients:**

- 2 ½ cups whole milk vanilla yogurt

- 1 ½ cups frozen peaches
- 1 cup frozen mango chunks
- ½ medium orange, zested

**Directions:**
1. Layer an 8" × 8" baking pan with parchment paper. Spread yogurt onto pan. Place yogurt in freezer at least 4 hours or overnight.
2. Remove from freezer and break into big chunks with a fork.
3. In a food processor, combine yogurt, peaches, mango, and orange zest. Pulse until a thick purée is made with fruit evenly distributed. Serve.

**Per serving:** Calories: 127kcal; Fat: 3.5g; Carbs: 20.6g; Protein: 3.9g

## 147. Almond Butter Fudge

**Preparation time:** 5 minutes
**Cooking time:** 7 minutes
**Servings:** 9 pieces
**Ingredients:**

- For the chocolate-honey sauce:
- 3 tablespoons cocoa powder
- 1½ tablespoons raw honey
- 3 tablespoons coconut oil
- Sea salt, to taste
- For the fudge:
- ¼ cup coconut oil
- 2 tablespoons coconut sugar
- ½ teaspoon vanilla extract
- 1 cup natural almond butter
- ½ teaspoon salt

**Directions:**
To make the chocolate-honey sauce:
1. Put the ingredients for the chocolate sauce in a saucepan and heat over medium heat for almost 5 minutes or until the sauce is lightly thickened. Keep stirring during the heating.
2. Remover the pan from the heat and let the mixture sit in a suitable bowl until ready to use.

To make the fudge:
3. Layer a loaf pan with parchment paper.
4. Melted the coconut oil in the cleaned saucepan over medium heat.
5. Turn off the heat then mix in the coconut sugar. Pour them in a separate bowl.
6. Add the rest of the ingredients and stir to combine well.
7. Pour the prepared mixture in the loaf pan, then put in the freezer to freeze for almost 15 minutes or until solid.
8. Remove the fudge from the freezer, then cut into 9 pieces and baste with sauce to serve.

**Per serving:** Calories: 337kcal; Fat: 29.4g; Carbs: 7.7g; Protein: 11.6g

## 148. Berry And Chia Yogurt

**Preparation time:** 10 minutes
**Cooking time:** 5 minutes
**Servings:** 4
**Ingredients:**

- 1 (10-ounce) package frozen mixed berries, thawed
- 2 tablespoons lemon juice
- ½ vanilla bean, halved lengthwise
- 2 tablespoons pure maple syrup
- 1 tablespoon chia seeds
- 4 cups almond yogurt

**Directions:**
1. Combine the mixed berries, lemon juice, vanilla bean, and maple syrup in a saucepan. Bring to a boil over medium-high heat. Stir constantly.
2. Reduce its heat to low and simmer for almost 3 minutes.

3. Turn off the heat, then discard the vanilla bean. Mix in the chia seeds, then let sit for almost 10 minutes or until the seeds are thickened.
4. Divide them into four serving bowls, then pour 1 cup of yogurt in each bowl. Serve immediately.

**Per serving:** Calories: 172kcal; Fat: 8.1g; Carbs: 25.5g; Protein: 4.1g

### 149. Blueberry Coconut Muffins

**Preparation time:** 5 minutes
**Cooking time:** 20 minutes
**Servings:** 4
**Ingredients:**

- ½ cup fresh blueberries
- 3 egg whites
- 1 tablespoon coconut flour
- 1 cup chickpea flour
- 1 tablespoon nutmeg, grated
- 1 teaspoon baking powder
- 1 teaspoon vanilla extract
- 1 teaspoon stevia

**Directions:**

1. At 325 degrees F, preheat your oven. Layer a 4-cup muffin tin with paper muffin cups.
2. Combine all the ingredients in a suitable bowl. Stir to mix well.
3. Divide the batter into the muffin cups, then set the muffin tin in the preheated oven.
4. Bake for almost 15 minutes or until a toothpick inserted in the center comes out clean.
5. Transfer the muffins on a cooling rack to cool for a few minutes before serving.

**Per serving:** Calories: 234kcal; Fat: 4.1g; Carbs: 37.2g; Protein: 13.1g

### 150. Figs Apple Compote

**Preparation time:** 1 hour
**Cooking time:** 5 minutes
**Servings:** 8
**Ingredients:**

- 4 cups apples, peeled and sliced
- 2 cups dried apricots, chopped
- 2 cups black figs, chopped
- 2 cups peaches, chopped
- 2 cups dates, chopped
- Juice of 1 lemon

**Directions:**

1. Put all the fruits in a suitable pot, then pour in enough water to cover.
2. Soak for an hour, then turn on the heat and bring to a boil.
3. Reduce its heat to low and simmer for almost 5 minutes.
4. Turn off the heat and drizzle with lemon juice.
5. Transfer them in a suitable bowl and serve immediately.

**Per serving:** Calories: 297kcal; Fat: 1.1g; Carbs: 75.1g; Protein: 3.1g

# CHAPTER 8: 30-Day Meal Plan

| Days | Breakfast | Lunch | Dinner | Dessert |
|---|---|---|---|---|
| 1 | Banana Coconut Pancakes | Quinoa With Pepperoncini | Beef Tenderloin | Blueberry Cobbler |
| 2 | Raspberry Pineapple Smoothie | Chicken Stir-Fry | Lemon Dill Salmon | Quinoa With Raspberries |
| 3 | Tofu Scramble | Mustard Pork Tenderloin | Thai Vegetable Soup | Almond Butter Mini Muffins |
| 4 | Artichoke Egg Casserole | Seared Cod With Mushroom Sauce | Coconut Lime Chicken With Cauliflower | Almond-Orange Torte |
| 5 | Broccoli Spinach Frittatas | Sweet Potato Leek Soup | Herbed Meatballs | Apple Cinnamon Muesli |
| 6 | Raspberry Oatmeal Bars | Turkey Kale Fry | Buckwheat Ramen With Cod | Strawberry Granita |
| 7 | Pumpkin Porridge | Bolognese Sauce | Cauliflower Rice Risotto | Banana Cacao Brownies |
| 8 | Tomatoes Egg Scramble | Garlic Shrimp And Broccoli | Chicken And Cauliflower Bake | Chocolate Tofu Pudding |
| 9 | Triple Berry Oats | Stuffed Sweet Potatoes | Beefy Lentil Stew | Chia Pudding With Cherries |
| 10 | Overnight Muesli | Lime Chicken And Rice | Shrimp Balls Over Garlicky Greens | Brownies With Strawberry Sauce |
| 11 | Black Bean Breakfast | Chili-Lime Pork Loin | Spiced Sweet Potato Soup | Glazed Pears With Hazelnuts |
| 12 | Blueberry Quinoa Porridge | Seared Citrus Scallops With Mint And Basil | Chicken Cacciatore | Banana Pops |
| 13 | Sweet Potato Orange Smoothie | Wild Rice Mushroom Soup | Beef Meatloaf | Chocolate Bark |
| 14 | Apple-Cinnamon Smoothie | Chicken Breasts With Mushrooms | Herbed Salmon Orzo Antipasto | Berry Pops |
| 15 | Coconut Chocolate Oatmeal | Beef And Bell Pepper Fajitas | Mushroom Risotto | Chai Pudding |
| 16 | Sweet Potato Casserole | Mediterranean Fish Stew | Spiced Chicken Vegetables | Ginger Jam Dots |
| 17 | Almond Granola | Vegetable Broth | Turkey Burgers | Blueberry Coconut Muffins |
| 18 | Pistachio Smoothie | Tuscan Chicken | Tuna Salad With | Chocolate Tofu |

|    |                               |                               | Brown Rice                        | Pudding                     |
|----|-------------------------------|-------------------------------|-----------------------------------|-----------------------------|
| 19 | Orange Oatmeal Muffins        | Beef Broth                    | Split Pea Carrot Soup             | Blueberry Cobbler           |
| 20 | Poppy Oatmeal Cups            | Power Poke Bowl               | Avocado Chicken Salad             | Quinoa With Raspberries     |
| 21 | Fruity Breakfast Bars         | Grain-Free Salad Bowl         | Fried Beef And Broccoli           | Berry And Chia Yogurt       |
| 22 | Spicy Quinoa                  | Whole Roasted Chicken         | Basic Shrimp                      | Spice Stuffed Apple Bake    |
| 23 | Coconut Pancakes              | Pork Ragù                     | Coconutty Brown Rice              | Peach-Raspberry Crumble     |
| 24 | Coconut Strawberry Porridge   | Shrimp Paella                 | Easy Chicken And Broccoli         | Mango-Peach Yogurt          |
| 25 | Apple Cinnamon Oats           | Basic Quinoa                  | Rosemary Chicken                  | Figs Apple Compote          |
| 26 | Turkey Hash                   | Gingered Turkey Meatballs     | Rainbow Trout                     | Almond-Orange Torte         |
| 27 | Banana Oatmeal                | Turkey Sweet Potato Hash      | Minestrone Soup                   | Apple Cinnamon Muesli       |
| 28 | Banana Date Porridge          | Seafood Stew                  | Chicken, Mushrooms, And Quinoa    | Strawberry Granita          |
| 29 | Beef Breakfast                | Baked Navy Beans              | Turkey Meatloaf                   | Coconut Hot Chocolate       |
| 30 | Pancake Bites                 | Italian Seasoned Turkey Breast| Hamburgers                        | Almond Butter Fudge         |

# Conclusion

Gout is a distressing condition. It's essential to keep in mind, though, that you can still cook your favorite meals. Be sure to consult your doctor before creating any dietary changes, and ensure these recipes are simultaneously healthy for you.

Gout may not be a manageable condition to handle, but you can do it with the correct information. A diet needs to be set up, and you need to have a few procedures, which is where this book steps in. The recipes found in the pages above are a good starter for a diet that will help to prevent and control your gout attacks.

Feel free to keep experimenting with different components, though. A diet doesn't have to be boring under any circumstances, particularly since the approaches for gout allow a vast range of components, from whole grains to eggs, vegetables & fruits. That is all you require for a healthy lifestyle and a fun and tasty kitchen repertoire. Just be open-minded & remain positive.

I hope this book was able to help you to know which foods are permitted or not for people afflicted with gout & discover how to prepare the recipes featured in this book.

# Index

Almond Butter Fudge; 69
Almond Butter Mini Muffins; 63
Almond Granola; 13
Almond-Orange Torte; 63
Apple Cinnamon Muesli; 63
Apple Cinnamon Oats; 14
Apple-Cinnamon Smoothie; 16
Artichoke Egg Casserole; 17
Avocado Chicken Salad; 42
Baked Navy Beans; 28
Baked Spiced Tofu; 25
Banana Cacao Brownies; 65
Banana Coconut Pancakes; 15
Banana Date Porridge; 16
Banana Oatmeal; 14
Banana Pops; 67
Basic Quinoa; 24
Basic Shrimp; 31
Bean Salsa; 58
Beef And Bell Pepper Fajitas; 52
Beef Breakfast; 19
Beef Broth; 50
Beef Meatloaf; 52
Beef Steak Tacos; 55
Beef Tenderloin; 53
Beefy Lentil Stew; 51
Berry And Chia Yogurt; 70
Berry Pops; 67
Black Bean Breakfast; 22
Blueberry Cobbler; 64
Blueberry Coconut Muffins; 70
Blueberry Quinoa Porridge; 18
Boiled Beans; 23
Bolognese Sauce; 54
Broccoli Spinach Frittatas; 12
Brownies With Strawberry Sauce; 66
Brussels Sprouts With Walnuts; 60
Buckwheat Ramen With Cod; 36
Butter Chickpeas; 26
Cauliflower Rice Risotto; 28
Cauliflower Rice With Beans; 56
Chai Pudding; 64
Chia Pudding With Cherries; 66

Chicken Adobo; 41
Chicken And Cauliflower Bake; 47
Chicken Bell Pepper Sauté; 49
Chicken Breasts With Mushrooms; 39
Chicken Cacciatore; 41
Chicken Sandwiches With Roasted Red Pepper Aioli; 46
Chicken Stir-Fry; 44
Chicken Tenders With Mustard Sauce; 39
Chicken, Mushrooms, And Quinoa; 48
Chickpea Smash; 56
Chili-Lime Pork Loin; 50
Chocolate Bark; 68
Chocolate Tofu Pudding; 68
Cinnamon Applesauce; 61
Citrus Spinach; 62
Coconut Chocolate Oatmeal; 17
Coconut Hot Chocolate; 65
Coconut Lime Chicken With Cauliflower; 45
Coconut Pancakes; 23
Coconut Strawberry Porridge; 15
Coconutty Brown Rice; 26
Cucumber And Bulgur Salad; 57
Easy Chicken And Broccoli; 45
Fennel Cabbage Slaw; 61
Figs Apple Compote; 71
Flaxseed Power Bites; 59
Fried Beef And Bell Pepper; 50
Fried Beef And Broccoli; 52
Fried Quinoa; 31
Fruity Breakfast Bars; 16
Garlic Shrimp And Broccoli; 38
Garlic Turkey Breast; 48
Ginger Jam Dots; 62
Gingered Turkey Meatballs; 43
Glazed Pears With Hazelnuts; 69
Grain-Free Salad Bowl; 29
Green Smoothie Bowl; 56
Ground Beef Chili With Tomatoes; 51
Ground Turkey And Spinach Stir-Fry; 47
Hamburgers; 53
Harvest Rice; 28
Herbed Meatballs; 54

Herbed Salmon Orzo Antipasto; 35
Italian Seasoned Turkey Breast; 46
Jerk Chicken; 40
Lemon Dill Salmon; 33
Lime Chicken And Rice; 49
Mango-Peach Yogurt; 69
Maple Collard Greens; 58
Mediterranean Fish Stew; 32
Minestrone Soup; 24
Mushroom Risotto; 31
Mustard Pork Tenderloin; 54
Orange Oatmeal Muffins; 15
Overnight Muesli; 23
Pancake Bites; 20
Peach-Raspberry Crumble; 62
Pickled Shiitake; 58
Pickled Vegetables; 55
Pico De Gallo; 61
Pistachio Smoothie; 12
Poppy Oatmeal Cups; 18
Pork Ragù; 51
Power Poke Bowl; 33
Pumpkin Porridge; 18
Quinoa With Pepperoncini; 24
Quinoa With Raspberries; 66
Rainbow Trout; 36
Raspberry Oatmeal Bars; 12
Raspberry Pineapple Smoothie; 19
Rosemary Chicken; 40
Seafood Stew; 35
Seared Citrus Scallops With Mint And Basil; 34
Seared Cod With Mushroom Sauce; 34

Shrimp Balls Over Garlicky Greens; 37
Shrimp Paella; 37
Spaghetti Squash; 27
Spanish Rice; 30
Spice Stuffed Apple Bake; 65
Spiced Chicken Vegetables; 40
Spiced Sweet Potato Soup; 25
Spicy Quinoa; 21
Split Pea Carrot Soup; 30
Strawberry Granita; 68
Stuffed Sweet Potatoes; 30
Sweet Potato Casserole; 19
Sweet Potato Leek Soup; 27
Sweet Potato Mash; 60
Sweet Potato Orange Smoothie; 14
Thai Vegetable Soup; 26
Toasted Nut Mix; 59
Tofu Scramble; 21
Tomatoes Egg Scramble; 22
Triple Berry Oats; 20
Tuna Salad With Brown Rice; 32
Turkey Burgers; 49
Turkey Hash; 13
Turkey Kale Fry; 47
Turkey Meatloaf; 42
Turkey Sweet Potato Hash; 44
Turkey With Bell Peppers And Rosemary; 43
Tuscan Chicken; 43
Vegetable Broth; 29
Whole Roasted Chicken; 44
Wild Rice Mushroom Soup; 27
Yogurt With Dates; 57
Zucchini Fritters; 57

Made in the USA
Middletown, DE
31 August 2024